SO GOOD, SO GOOD, SO GOOD! CONFESSIONS OF THE PIANO DUDE

A Memoire of Cruise Ship Life, Serial Rapists, Becoming Minimalist, Finding Love, and Living the Dream

Gregg Akkerman

Book #3 in the *Awesome Music is Your Business* Series

Cover designed by Tehsin Gull (fairy@99 at 99designs.com)
Cover photo by Roy Mezzapelle

For more content, visit http://greggakkerman.com/
Follow Gregg Akkerman on Facebook at Gregg the Writer

Print version ISBN-13: 9781797889818

"Life is like a tambourine:
the more you shake it,
the better it seems."
—Robert Plant

CONTENTS

ACKNOWLEDGEMENTS

ENDLESS GRATITUDE in hindsight for the profoundly influential words expressed to me from two women with foresight:

Marillyn (or as I call her, Mom) in 1972: "Get in the car—I signed you up for piano lessons." I was mortified at the time, but still thank her on a regular basis.

Kathy in 2017: "I do." No sweeter words have my ears heard.

And from a few good men:

Brother Dave explaining improvisation to me when we were teens: "Just play what you want." He pretty much nailed it.

Don (Dad): "I love you and I'm proud of you." How many sons never get to hear that?

Anonymous guy in a piano bar: "What do you call that style of playing—slap and tickle?" I do now.

DISCLAIMER

EVERYTHING IN THIS BOOK is written with an intention of truthiness. If you were there and remember it differently, you have my apologies. Now go and write your own damn book.

INTRODUCTION: WHY?

TO BE HONEST, I get tired of answering all the same questions: How long have you been playing? Where'd you get your start? Can I give you a back rub? I'll just put it all down in one place and say, "Buy my book, and a little lower to the left."

What follows are a series of vignettes, each representing a poignant moment of my life as a musician and Dude on a path to being less of a dumbass. Some of the chapters are just for kicks, while others are more serious, but it's been a heck of a great ride so far. If I'm not living a charmed life, it'll do until the real thing comes along.

CHAPTER 1: THE PIANO IS

IT HAS ALWAYS BEEN THERE.

In my youngest days crawling—a place to hide.

During my furtive early steps—a sharp edge to my soft head.

While tethered to Mom as a toddler—a cozy bench to sit next to her.

For my single-digit years—the wellspring of storytelling fascination.

As a pre-teen—the chore to be completed.

With changes in my body—a portal to explore both inward and outward.

To a teenager seeking identity—a means to both belong and rebel.

In the aspiring eyes of a young man—a possible way out.

In the placenta of a career's birth—a source of sustenance.

During the years of mastery—a challenge accepted.

As the years rolled by—the only constant.

And finally—the friend who knows...everything.

Age 1 with the family piano

CHAPTER 2: WEDNESDAYS WITH MRS. PERVUS

"I WON'T TELL YOU AGAIN, now GET IN THE CAR!" At the time I heard this command I was an eight-year-old boy on the receiving end of his mother's scowl. All my delaying tactics had failed. It was now inevitable. I was going for my first piano lesson and was not happy about it. I'd heard the stories from other boys at school: knuckles rapped with rulers; having to wear a tie and stiff shoes at recitals; and the fate worse than death—being forced to play duets with silly girls covered in poufy dresses. Mom now had me in her clutches, and as she strapped me in the family Ford Pinto station-wagon I prepared for what was sure to be the worst day of my life.

As we pulled into the driveway of our destination the previous hour's hapless victim was walking out to a waiting car. The grin on his face didn't fool me for an instant. It had to be a clever ruse to hide the horrors of what was surely inflicted upon him every week. I walked to the door to be greeted by a thin, charcoal-eyed, colorful shirt-wearing woman that was older than Mom but younger than Grandma. She smiled, pat me on the head, and complemented my manners—I hated her already. As I entered the living room, I faced immediate and thorough inspection by a succession of four dogs, each bigger than the previous. Being found clean of explosives I was allowed to proceed to the piano bench.

In an obvious attempt to lull me into her web of musical torture I was told to, "Be a dear and play a little something." With one eye on my antagonist, one on the keys, and two feet dangling, I began to play the only song I knew:

Mar-y had a lit-tle "*oops*," lit-tle "*darn*," lit-"*fudge*" lamb
Mar-y "*rats*" a "*doh*"-tle lamb, her "*grrr*" was white as "*arrrgh!*"

Wow, that was the best I'd ever played that song! "Not bad," I thought. "Any intelligent adult will certainly realize I don't need lessons when I have already mastered all the nuances of Mary and her Lamb." I proudly turned to Mom for confirmation, but instead found her digging a checkbook from her purse as she said, "I suppose we'd better pay for the whole month up front."

The next four years I spent 30 minutes nearly every Wednesday at 4:30 PM with Mrs. Pervus and her four dogs. Some days her 5 PM victim might have even seen me walk out to the car with a slight grin on my face.

CHAPTER 3: I MET MY WIFE WHEN WE WERE ELEVEN

[*This chapter opens with a guest writer, my wife Kathy, as she recounts our early story—she tells it way better than I do.*]

It was March of 1978. I went to the elementary school multipurpose-room during recess to see if the band director was there. The room was dark, but I could hear someone playing piano, so I quietly snuck in and followed the sound. I could see this cute, little, strawberry-blond-headed boy playing the "Pink Panther" theme, of all things, which totally captivated me. It was a swingin' tune back in '78. I stood in the dark and watched him for quite a while—mesmerized. I just wanted to watch him play without revealing myself. But he realized someone was nearby—I was caught.

You and I must have said some youthful "hello's" and introduced ourselves, and by the end of our 10 minutes together we were chasing each other around the building playing tag, which is an eleven-year-old's version of flirting I suppose.

We spent the next few days accidentally-on-purpose sidling up next to each other at recess and I was definitely interested. You were so adorable. Soon, the word was out across the playground that you were going to ask to "go steady" with me. The next morning was Saint Patrick's Day, so I put on my favorite green shirt, and at recess I made sure I was in the same area of the playground as you. Right before the bell sounded you walked up and popped your question. I said, "YES!" and quickly ran away. But that was the start of something beautiful.

A schoolmate chided me that "you're not really boyfriend-girlfriend unless you kiss." Kids of that era had an amazing gossip network that worked as fast as any modern texting, and the message spread like lightning: "Today is the day they're gonna kiss; by the handball court!" So, I knew the when and the where. I just had to summon my courage to go kiss my first boy. I was there, you were there, and other kids were milling around to see if anything interesting would happen. I was looking away and when I turned back you were RIGHT THERE, and it was the quickest little thing when our lips touched. Once again, I ran away as fast as I could, but that kiss was worth it!

A sad day was at the end of that school year when I knew I would be moving to the neighboring school district. Being pre-internet, it might as well have been across the country because kids in different school districts seldom interacted. You walked me to the school bus stop and we signed each other's yearbooks. We both used the word "love" in our signatures which was pretty sophisticated for our age, but you didn't really say much. The bus drove me away and we waved goodbye thinking we'd never see each other again. Who knew it would all have such a profound meaning to us decades later?

♦ ♦ ♦

Gregg Continues the Story...

It came to me in a dream. It was so obvious. How could I have not thought of it already? I knew just how I would propose to Kathy. But let me back up...

In early 2014, I received a Facebook friend request from Kathy Harris. I wasn't sure of the name, but I certainly recognized the picture—that was a grown-up version of the cute, little girl from elementary school! Young Kathy Crippen had become a lovely adult woman. We soon exchanged the perfunctory benchmarks regarding the current status of marriage, kids, family, and jobs. Much to our surprise, our mothers lived no more than a mile apart, and we discussed visiting with each other when we were both in that area.

In the fall, I was home with Mom after my first contract as a cruise-ship piano bar entertainer and busy promoting my just-released book on Led Zeppelin. Kathy reached out that she would be visiting her mom for a few days so we arranged a time to meet and she could get a signed copy. We had an absolutely fine evening playing catch-up and laughing about all things great and small.

I found Kathy to be wonderful and compatible company. We had both pursued music as a career. We both had gone to college for music study and eventually earned graduate degrees. Like her mother and both of my parents (and me for a decade), she was an educator. We had even both taken major steps in recent years to get healthy and lose weight. It showed in her slim-fitting jeans.

My schoolyard crush had grown up to be one hell of a woman. To me, she seemed like a happy wife, a good mom to two kids, and a seasoned pro as a school band teacher. As it turned out, I got two out of three right.

We saw each other a few more times around the holidays before I left for a second cruise ship contract in Australia. I was consistently impressed at how committed she was to making time to see me when she was in the area. She was always on time, never cancelled for murky reasons, and was very "present" while we were together.

Even though Kathy and I weren't seeing each other romantically, this was a stark contrast to the woman I was sorta-kinda involved with at the time who often fell short of those attributes. Kathy and I now humorously refer to this as our period of going on "non-dates" with each other.

While I was gone on my 5-month contract, Kathy and I engaged in what was essentially old-fashioned letter writing, except in email form. Anyone who has worked far from home for months at a time knows how important getting mail is, and Kathy wrote often. It meant a lot to me, and there was an obvious closeness developing.

Eventually, Kathy admitted her marriage was ready to formally dissolve after 25 years. As happens so often, there was an attempt to keep the peace while the kids were still home, but that phase was soon to end...and then what?

Several more months passed while her separation and divorce proceeded, and I detached from the other relationship I had been trying to nurture. By the holidays of 2015, we were emotionally available and began dating as a couple.

When her son asked what the family was doing together for New Year's Eve, Kathy officially outed us by declaring, "I don't know about you, but I'VE got a date!" Deliriously giddy most all the time, we were pretty much insufferable to everyone around us, but didn't care. We both deserved the relationship we were giving each other and reveled in the joy of it all.

By the next fall, we had already begun talking marriage and wedding rings. I let her know I was onboard, but didn't want to proceed until we knew her divorce was behind us. She was told it would be complete before Christmas. By Thanksgiving, we had the rings in our possession, and a wedding date picked for Saturday, July 29, 2017 (both our birthdays fall on a 29th). But how to propose? That was now the enormously stressful question for me.

I pondered some of the usual formats but nothing struck me as uniquely "us," and I wanted something better for my schoolyard crush when she became my betrothed.

... and then...it came to me in a dream. It was so obvious. How could I have not thought of it already? I knew just how I would propose to Kathy. It would happen on New Year's Eve while we were elegantly dressed for an evening out celebrating the anniversary of our first official date. I knew just the perfect spot where I would have the perfect words to say before hearing her perfect response! I even drove to the location ahead of time to make sure it was accessible at night. Everything checked out.

A couple nights before "the night," we were sitting together on the sofa when we got some welcomed news that had been delayed by several days. Kathy's divorce was finalized! We greeted the life-changing proclamation with a toast, and cheered our bright future together. And just then it occurred to me...this was also a 29th—*that date ties everything together!* THE PROPOSAL HAS TO BE TONIGHT! But I didn't have the perfect words memorized yet because I thought I still had two days. I was wearing jeans, she was wearing sweats, I hadn't shaved, and she wasn't wearing much makeup. What to do?

"Kathy, I need you to trust me and get in the car. It's important." While she got her coat, I slipped the ring into my pocket, and off we went. This was happening.

From our home, I drove us west on Highway 111 for a few miles. Kathy's mind was furiously processing what was going on, but she stayed mostly quiet while she let me have my moment. I passed a couple landmarks she might have thought we were aiming for before we approached the old neighborhood. By the time I turned left on Indian Trail Road, she had pieced it together, and sensed how absolutely ideal it was.

A few more blocks and the scattered collection of buildings rose out of the darkness as our headlights brought Rancho Mirage Elementary School into view where it all began in 1978. There was the multi-purpose room where we said our first tentative "hello" around the piano. There was the schoolyard where we first kissed by the handball court. There was the driveway for the busses to take little girls away on the last day of school. And there was the sidewalk for awkward little boys to stand who don't know how to say goodbye.

It was that exact spot I parked the car, came around to open Kathy's door, and helped to her feet as I walked us to where I would have stood almost 39 years earlier. Then, on bended knee, I nervously presented the best argument I could think of under abbreviated circumstances for her marrying me:

> *"I brought you here to right a wrong. I should have never let you get on the bus that day without telling you how I felt about us. I hope you'll allow me to atone for that mistake. Will you be my wife?"*

Without any hesitation, the first word from Kathy's lips was a glorious, "YES!" My childhood sweetheart had become the love of my life and soon would be my wife. I'm pretty sure I heard the echoing of bells from the surrounding hills. It was all perfect, just the way it happened.

Age 11, school band with Kathy

CHAPTER 4: WAIT, CHICKS DIG MUSICIANS?

FINALLY, THE HOUSE WAS EMPTY, so I could have that private time all teenaged boys look for. I couldn't wait to surround myself with a few of my favorite centerfolds spread out on the floor around me. However, in my world, this meant staring dreamily not at girly magazines but at the images of classic "gatefold" albums from rock groups like Yes, Pink Floyd, Led Zeppelin, Jeff Beck, Rush, and Emerson, Lake and Palmer.

I'd slowly ease the vinyl from the slip cover and place it on the turntable. Then with great care, the needle would be dropped at the beginning of side one. I never understood how some of my friends only wanted to hear a single song somewhere in the middle of an LP record. To me, if you liked a band, you listened to the whole album because every song mattered in the order they were presented.

As the music began to emerge from the speakers—back when the "home stereo" was a major feature of the living room—I would dim the lights, take my place at the piano, and do my best to play along with those most revered of songs.

"Roundabout," "Karn Evil 9," "Tom Sawyer," "No Quarter," "Freeway Jam," "Shine on You Crazy Diamond;" these were my inspirational teachers and mentors. From them I learned about polyrhythms, advanced chords, proper fingering, instrumentation, song form, and the difference between good and great music.

Sitting there in the dark, struggling to keep up with the music I heard, I was never a more committed musician than at any time in my life. Those were the glorious years of innocence, ignorance, and hope. I likely played as many wrong notes as right ones, but I was never a more creative soul than in those youthful moments of unchecked imagination, surrounded by record covers, and existing purely in the moment.

♦ ♦ ♦

My years at junior and senior high school were a musical dichotomy: I had a "home" life of rock music and piano, and a school life of band and saxophone. Rarely did the two mingle. In fact, the piano side almost got killed off early in the running. After taking lessons from the kindly neighborhood lady for four years, I convinced Mom that I had served my time and deserved to be released from the confines of a piano bench.

I was weary from playing pieces I'd never heard of by long-dead European composers. The final straw was when I played a movement of a Beethoven sonata for a competition recital and was marked down for tapping the beat with my foot. That was basically the end of my stint performing classical piano. Old Ludwig simply couldn't compete with the power of "Kashmir" coming through my stereo.

Meanwhile, I had begun playing saxophone in the 5th grade and by the time I got to Nellie N. Coffman Junior High the music director needed an alto player for the stage band (this was the label schools came up with back in the 1950s because "jazz band" was considered too black). I was the only 7th grader in the band full of older kids so I had to kick up my game and try to be "cool."

The biggest advantage to being in the stage band wasn't revealed to me until after our first lunch-time performance. I was told by a few giggling classmates that I was thought to be "cute" by some girls watching the show.

Girls noticed me and I didn't have to do anything but be on a stage doing something I already liked? Yup. Not only that, but in the coming days I noticed more kids were saying hi to me on a regular basis. Just like that, I had become "popular" simply by playing 2nd alto sax in the stage band.

It turns out the rumors were true—chicks dig musicians! As long as I was holding my sax, I could just stand against a wall and girls would talk to me. For someone who often felt out of sync with people and kids around me, what a gold mine I had inadvertently stepped into. This was going to need more research on my part.

"Hey Mom? I've been thinking—maybe I should start taking piano lessons again, but maybe we could find a teacher who knows something about jazz or rock." That query led to four more years of lessons and considerably more evidence that music was indeed a great way to meet new friends and learn more about myself.

Unknown to most of my schoolmates as I was promoted to Palm Springs High School, I kept plugging away at my "home" music life. The concept of "garage band" doesn't really exist in the desert where I grew up because garages are hot, but my select teen pals managed to find spaces to form our first attempts at rock stardom.

The most common place to jam was somebody's living room while the adults were still at work. That's where my earliest rocker cohorts and I would bash away at the likes of "Satisfaction," "Whole Lotta Love," and "Smoke on the Water."

What a magnificent racket we made with borrowed instruments, out-of-tune guitars, little knowledge of how to actually play, and no proper PA system. Yet every minute of it was flipping brilliant! Let the jocks and preps have their sports and school clubs—we knew the real beauty of the world could be found in those living rooms pounding two or three chords and believing with certainty that rock music would save us all. It was true for some of us. Damn, those were good days.

CHAPTER 5: GETTING NAKED WITH THE CHIEFTAINS

MY DAD COULD TALK to anybody. He was fearless when it came to shaking hands and chatting it up with new people. This made him the life of a party, or on one particular occasion, the cause of a party.

"Gregg, come on over to Hemet this weekend, and bring your keyboard—you know, that big one you've got."

Dad knew my weakness. Ask me to bring my "suitcase" Fender Rhodes to make some music and I'm there. He loved to jam on classic country (Hank Williams SENIOR), could strum a guitar just fine, and had a smooth, pitch-perfect singing voice. Some of the best music I've ever played was "Watermelon Wine" with Dad and his cohorts getting together for a potluck and hootenanny.

"Sure man. What's the occasion?" I asked him.

"Oh, you never know," he said with a hint of gleeful evasion.

Sure enough, come Friday afternoon I packed up the four-door Chevy Citation hatchback with my gear, a brand-new Night Ranger cassette, and a couple clean shirts. After putting a little bit of Interstate 10 and Lambs Canyon behind me, there I was at the horse-ranch home of Dad and my Step-Mom which they had built up from the dirt some years before. I let myself into the backyard and heard the familiar paternal voice:

"Hey there! Don't get too comfortable. We're going to over to the community college for a concert. I got tickets for some band from Ireland that sound like fun." That was Dad—always on the lookout for some new people to meet.

At the time, I had never heard of "The Chieftains," and it would be years before I heard of them again and started to put it all together. At that point, they had already been together for nearly twenty years, were a major act in Europe, and within another year broke a cultural barrier by performing several concerts along the Great Wall of China. But that night, amid the chill of late-fall in small-town southern California, they were an unknown entity touring college campuses in a single van.

I recall the music as being exotic, playful, and at times a little moody. As a teenage Tolkien loyalist, I could easily imagine the melodies and harmonies as a sonic backdrop to Hobbits and Elves (an association that would bear out decades later in the *Lord of the Rings* movies). As soon as their show ended was when my Dad's performance began. He promptly approached the musicians and crew:

"You fellas are terrific. So where are you staying in town? How about you come on back to my place? Cheaper than a motel and we'll have ourselves a little party 'round the pool."

That last word sealed the deal. To these guys from Ireland, a private, southern California swimming pool was a mythical unicorn, and they were not about to pass up the opportunity to see one for themselves.

Flash forward a couple hours, and there we all were in the backyard of Dad's ranch, instruments set up between the patio furniture, and I'm jammin' with the Chieftains who would go on to be nominated for eighteen Grammy awards and win six of them. Being from Europe, they were keenly interested in American music instruments, and the keyboardist in particular was fascinated by my electric piano. Suddenly, I had a new-found pride for what was moments before just a heavy, beat-up, cigarette-burned keyboard I had found in the classified ads of the *Press-Enterprise* newspaper. Turns out, it wasn't old and tattered but "vintage" and "care-worn." The "oohs" and "aahs" continued when my Dad brought out his 1972, cherry-red Gibson ES-335 guitar (like Roy Orbison used) and a Fender speaker cabinet with the beige covering. Now it was the guitarist's turn to be awestruck.

"Oh my, you've got yourself a beige!" he said with a profound mix of wonder and envy. It turns out that when said by an Irish musician with a couple pints already behind him, the word "beige" actually has three syllables: "bay-ee-zha." That's when I knew I was completely in love with these guys. I wanted to load up my rig and two shirts and travel with them the rest of my life.

I remember making a lot of pretty good music that night, but since I didn't think they were more than an Irish garage band, it never occurred to me to take any photos or make a recording. Whatever notes we put together were given up to the stars above and the cool breeze blowing down from San Jacinto Mountain.

As the evening progressed, and the beverages had their intended effect, the magnetic attraction of the pool became too much for these wandering troubadours to withstand. The roadie for the band was the first to crack.

“I’m goin’ in. Who’s with me?”

Not waiting for a response, he took it to the next level and began shedding layers of clothes. It was cold enough that we were all wearing coats, but he was on a mission and would not be denied. Standing in only his droopy boxer shorts, he gave a whelp and flung himself into the deep end.

He splished and splashed, called everyone cowards, and proceeded to have a glorious time. It worked. Clothes began flying in multiple directions. Shoes here, socks there, coats, shirts, and pants everywhere, all to be sorted out much later. Soon, a pile of us were in the pool singing and carrying on as if all the troubles of the world could be set aside for a while, and we were meant only to enjoy the company of new friends and new songs.

I was sixteen, I was immortal, and I was gettin’ naked with the Chieftains.

Age 16 loading the Fender Rhodes

CHAPTER 6: THE COVER-BAND WARRIOR

ONCE IN A WHILE THE QUESTION GETS RAISED at a house party, pub gathering, or a break between sets: "So what's the most embarrassing thing that ever happened to you on the job?"

The answer is always horribly vivid in my mind. I envision a day when I won't cringe at the very memory, but I doubt it will ever come until I am finally released.

I was a young man of 18 and had spent a few days in Walnut Creek, California visiting with a darling young lady and her family. The drive was shared with her grandparents who lived near me in southern California. The drive north was fine, but the return trip turned a bit grim.

The grandparents and I headed off early in the day to begin what was likely a 10-hour drive. It was only a few hours later during a late-morning stop at a rest area when events soured. Grandpa (as he kindly asked me to call him) became violently ill in the parking lot. As he told me days later, "Son, I think I threw up food I ate in second grade!"

It became clear that he could not continue all the way to the Inland Empire where I had a gig that night playing with a top-40 band in

Cathedral City. What happened next still impresses me to this day. They handed me the keys to their Cadillac, wrote down the entrance code to the home-security system, gave me some money for gas, and said, "You get on down the road. We'll rent a car tomorrow and be just fine."

I dropped that Caddy's hammer and pulled into Palm Springs to pick up my car, get my gear, and rush to the gig. I was just late enough that the band had to start the first song without me, but I rushed to set up my keyboard rig in record time. The guitarist thought he was going to have to play the keyboard solo in Scandal's "Goodbye to You," but no need: I came in on the second beat of the measure, right on time. Paul, the bass player, just looked at me with his big smile and rolled his eyes.

The band was called MYX. Admittedly, not a very unique moniker, but the name was easy to remember and served its purpose. We were a pretty good cover band; all five of us could sing which allowed for variety, and having a girl singer meant we could do material that all-male bands couldn't. Besides Scandal, there was Missing Persons, Berlin, Pat Benatar, Katrina and the Waves, the Motels, and my personal favorite 1980's trivia answer: Quarterflash.

The gig that night was in what by all definitions must be called a dive bar. Not a dump, mind you—just a highway roadhouse that served two kinds of beer: Miller or Miller Lite. The regular patrons were raucous but a generally friendly bunch, and that night they did me the greatest of favors by collectively ignoring what was soon to happen right there in front of them.

As the set proceeded, I felt myself perspiring much more than I normally do, even onstage. The room felt unbearably warm and I tugged at the various zippers on my parachute pants as they clung to my moist body. I called out over the loud music to Paul, "ARE YOU HOT?" To which he incoherently responded, "ABOUT NINE-THIRTY." He was no help.

Then things got really weird. The lights hurt my eyes. The sounds of the band crashed through my ears. My mind swirled within my tottering body. It dawned on me that I must have gotten the same bug as dear old Grandpa. And then it happened...up came everything! Second grade; first grade; heck, I'm sure there was some cheese and crackers from nursery school in there. And I was right on stage with nowhere to hide and nowhere to run.

The only saving grace to that instant of time was that an empty beer pitcher had been left near me on the stage, and I had just enough time to stick my face in it. So, there I was filling up some of the bar's finest plasticware while the dancers got their groove on to the band's attempt (being one man down) at ZZ-Top's "Sharp Dressed Man."

I staggered through the crowd and headed for the bathroom with my near-capacity receptacle and made it just in time to continue purging in relative solitude. Now, like I said, I consider this event to be the most embarrassing moment I ever experienced on the job, but I gotta tell you, it could have been so much worse. I could have been the brunt of jokes and ridicule that night and every gig I ever played in town for years to come. But instead, not one person ever said a word about it. Not ONE, except, "How you doin' there champ? Feeling any better?" Talk about giving a guy a break when he was down.

It was a hell of a tough night, but in the spirit of the times, I just had to harden my heart because I'm a real tough cookie with a long history after all this walkin' on sunshine even though nobody walks in L.A. and then suddenly last summer find that I am the warrior and still hungry like the wolf.

CHAPTER 7: COLLEGE GIRLS AND VICIOUS FISH

THE FIRST TIME I MET MY COLLEGE ROOMATE was in the fall of 1986. I had arrived at my San Diego State University dorm a couple days earlier to attend an orientation meeting, so by the time he arrived, I was anxious to know who I would be living with during my first year.

Unknown to me at the time, Mark, still only 17, had just finished a summer of boot camp and basic training for the Army and was still sporting his close-shaved haircut. Into our small room he stomped with his black marching boots, green soldier-pants, and sunglasses while packing in an enormous guitar amplifier with a lightning bolt and the word "OZ" stencil-painted on the front cover. I couldn't tell if he was a skinhead punk rocker or simply a scary looking trained killer. Either way, I knew I liked him straight off, especially when I learned we both liked falling asleep listening to a cassette tape of "The Wall" from Pink Floyd.

It wasn't long before Mark and I found a bass player down the hall of our dorm. Eric was a good-looking guy, a solid musician, and one hell of a beer drinker. That left only a drummer to find, and I had the answer in a desert buddy I had since 7th grade. As teens, we used to set up in whatever empty space we could find and jam for hours on tunes from Asia, Human League, and the Cure. Max had moved to

San Diego before I did and was game for joining the band we soon named "Vicious Fish." I thought of the name and liked the way it sounded when pronounced out loud.

With three of us living in a dorm, we needed a place to rehearse and found some inexpensive rehearsal studios in what was one of the dodgiest areas of town. As soon as we entered the parking lot, I noticed how the smell of cigarette smoke and urine was the perfect pairing to the sound of breaking bottles and sex for hire. The Midway District in San Diego was not the place to leave your car unlocked, but at 10 bucks an hour for rehearsal rooms, it was in the Vicious Fish budget.

Four or five rehearsals later, we had enough tunes ready for our public debut in the SDSU area. Being a nationally ranked top-3 party school meant there were always plenty of frat parties, and we were ready to snag our share. Max's roommate was on the "social committee" for his frat and arranged for us to play at their next keg party. Eric couldn't wait: "Dude, we'll get laid and drink for free!"

We had a pretty good set comprised of classics of the day by the Call, the Fix, the Kinks, the Kingsmen, and the Squeeze: all the great "The" bands. We even managed to write a few original songs to slip in among the popular party tunes.

Despite what we all assumed from watching *Animal House* a thousand times, frat parties are awesome to *attend* but a terribly messy place to *work*. Spilled beer on the bass amp, spilled beer in the guitar amp, spilled beer on the snare drum, and the synthesizer, and the sound system, and the microphones...you get the idea. Then came the drunk assholes flinging bodies into the drum set while their buddies yelled, "Strike!" or, "Gutter!" depending on how many cymbal stands were knocked over. Complete debauchery.

As for the prospect of sex, college always seemed to be a place where everyone got laid but me. I had my share of dates and lost weekends but at the time, I was better at understanding music than I was women. Music can be converted to numbers, and from there, any form of manipulation becomes possible. The only limit is imagination. But women? I certainly pursued them regularly and with conviction, but much like the neighborhood dog always chasing cars down the block, I didn't have much of a plan once I caught one.

The glory days of Vicious Fish were short-lived, but they were a brilliantly fun bump in the road and well worth the time. Mark is still married to the girl he met near the end of his SDSU days, and they are the parents of beautiful kids who probably have no idea what a rocking guitarist and party connoisseur their father was. Max and I are still friends after 40 years and counting; he's also married with gorgeous daughters. He and his lovely wife came to my wedding in 2017. And Eric...well, I have no idea, but I suspect he did just fine for himself. Party on, dudes.

Age 22 with Vicious Fish

CHAPTER 8: A WHITE GUY FROM PALM SPRINGS GETS THE BLUES

"YOU KNOW, I SHOULD INTRODUCE YOU to my buddy Todd who is a big-time blues guy here in town," said my new landlord, also named Todd. As is typical with college students, I needed a place to live for a semester and found a flyer on campus with Todd's number. He offered a room in his house with kitchen privileges, but the main appeal was that it was just a couple blocks from school so I avoided the parking problems at San Diego State University.

As I was moving in, Todd noticed all my various keyboard equipment and asked if I was into the blues. "Sure," I said, "Led Zeppelin's first album is one of my favorites." "Naw, man. I mean the BLUES!" he shot back. Okay, got it. Rock bands who play bluesy don't count. I tossed out the only name I could think of: "I've got a cassette of Howling Wolf that's pretty good." That's when he first mentioned the other Todd who could likely find paying work for a blues keyboardist, so I guess I passed his audition.

Even though I was on pace to soon complete my Bachelor of Arts in Psychology, I had already determined that I would commit myself to making a living as a musician as soon as I graduated. To prepare, I had been taking private lessons from a top jazz-rock-fusion keyboardist in Los Angeles and getting my chops up. I was feeling ready for the next step.

Todd #2 was a 350-pound, warm-hearted, fiercely dedicated blues fan who didn't play an instrument, so his way to be involved in the scene was as a promoter and manager. He quickly took me under his wing to educate me on blues greats. He would flip me mix-tapes (remember those?) of Professor Longhair, Dr. John, Jimmy Smith, Pinetop Perkins, and so many more. It was like being in a graduate course for blues piano, and I soaked it all in. He would pick me up in his piece of crap old Lincoln, piled high in burrito wrappers and cassette cases, and haul me around to the area venues, introducing me to the players and bar managers.

Eventually, Todd #2 set me up as the house keyboardist for a blues jam he hosted on Sunday nights at a joint in Ocean Beach. It was a noisy, brawling, working-class crowd, and I had a blast playing loud and applying all my studies.

The contacts I made through that first gig soon developed into enough steady work that by the time I graduated from SDSU, I was making just enough to support myself with music. Playing maybe 20 gigs a month brought in $1,000 under the table. Rent was $300, gas, car insurance, and food ate up another $500. Hell, I was living like a king with $200 to spare for beer, condoms, and poor decision making.

The timing was right too because I needed to move away from Todd #1. I was in the backyard once and he warned me to avoid the rat traps he set to kill wayward cats. He also mentioned how much he enjoyed working as a bouncer because he got to smash the teeth of drunks by placing their faces against a curb and stomping on the back of their heads.

I wasn't making big bucks yet, but for the first time in my life, I could say I was a professional musician. Eventually, I worked with some big southern California blues names like Debbie Davies, Juke Logan, and Ossie Anderson, and was the opening act for national acts like Koko Taylor, B.B. King, and Etta James. I may have grown up in the land of Palm Springs swimming pools, but I was pulling my weight as a San Diego bluesman and getting my groove on, even if I still thought Zep played some badass blues.

CHAPTER 9: MEETING THE KING

"GOOD NEWS GUYS, YOU GOT THE GIG opening for B.B." We'd been hoping to hear that announcement for weeks and congratulated ourselves for beating out the other San Diego-based blues bands gunning for the slot. It seemed the management at the Bacchanal nightclub finally realized we could outplay the competition.

And why not? The drummer, Bob, was always solid. A bit too easy to piss off, but it never kept him from playing a strong backbeat. The bassist, also named Bob, had great rhythm and the audiences always seemed amused by how he played with his mouth half open and jaw shoved off to the side like he was perpetually prepared to catch rain water. Our sax player was an ace mercenary in the local blues scene and wore the nickname "Roger Fucking Dodger" like a precious scar. He eventually left the group when he couldn't put up with the bandleader anymore. That leader, Junior, was our guitarist/vocalist out of Texas which gave him instant credibility as a more authentic bluesman than the rest of us could ever be. He was only an adequate singer which, unfortunately, matched his guitar chops, but he had a certain style and charm about him. He could win over hearts with a wink and a smile before we laid down the first twelve bars. And then there was the keyboardist—me. I willingly fulfilled the stereotype as the trained musician who over thought most things and threw a snit if rehearsals started ten minutes late. That was us in 1990, the *Junior Jackson Blues Band* and we were opening up for the greatest bluesman alive.

When word first spread that the Bacchanal would be booking the opening act for the B.B. King show all the local blues bands took note. We had yet to play that room so our manager quickly pulled some strings to get us the opening slot for a popular regional act, Coco Montoya. We did well enough that the club's booking manager gave us our own headliner gig on an off night.

For that show we worked our asses off to pull in all of our regular crowd from the small bars we usually played: Winston's, Patrick's II, the Sunset Grill, McDougal's Pub, Blind Melons, the Catamaran, Tuba Man's, Ingrid's Cantina, the Stadium Bar, and a few others that time has mercifully allowed me to forget.

Besides our regulars were the girlfriends. There was the older divorcee who took care of Junior and always brought a crowd of she-friends to admire her "special young man." The bass player had his steady lady that dressed like a Stevie Nicks yard sale. I once seriously asked her if she and Bob were witches and her response was, "Pretty much, yea, but Bob prefers the term warlock." Then, taking a hit off the reefer being passed around, she casually added, "Let me know if you ever want a threesome." Drummer-Bob's girlfriend was a lock to attend. She attended all our shows, got drunk and yelled at no one in particular how we were "so mush bedder 'an Canned Heat." With no steady girlfriend at the time, I did my best to encourage a crew of rowdies from my recent stint at San Diego State University to make the show. They could usually be counted on to ring up an impressive bar tab.

Through our combined efforts we managed to bring in a good-sized crowd that night and from the moment we were introduced as "kickin' ass and takin' names," we swung hard for the fences. When the set was over and the crowd called out for more, Junior turned to us with that sweet grin and said, "The gig with B.B. is ours, boys. Now let's send 'em home wet." Then, loud enough for all to hear, "CHICAGO SHUFFLE, FAST FOUR, HOUSE KEY, a-ONE, TWO, THREE, FOUR..." Loud and proud, baby.

A couple days later our manager told us it was a done deal—the gig was ours! "Not much money," he added, "but the house sound man will set us up with his best gear and we can even use the Hammond B-3 being brought in special for B.B.'s keyboardist." For a broke, just-out-of-college kid like me this was huge. The B-3 organ is legendary and to that point I had only ever seen a couple and never gotten to play one. I frothed at the thought of sitting in front of those dual keyboards, foot pedals, and a console full of dials and sliders—devastating power at my fingertips.

We refined our set over the next couple weeks at our regular beach-bar gig. For bands like ours, that was our music school. That was where we honed our trade. That gig and the dozens before it was where we earned the right to play in front of the man named Blues Boy King.

The night arrived—both shows were sold out. In our dressing room just before taking the stage, drummer-Bob, already a six-pack in, got annoyed by something forgettable and told our manager to screw himself. Yup, everything was happening right on schedule. We came out to bright lights and a steamy, cheering crowd.

I saw hundreds of unknown faces mixed with a handful of familiar ones: crossed-armed guitarists in the front row with their "you ain't so hot" stares; the girlfriends at the tables just off to the side trying not to look too obvious in their new black boots; dudes I knew from the beach bars grudgingly handing over cash for overpriced beer; single chicks in spaghetti-stringed halter tops I'd have a slight chance to meet up with later, and one or two I never should have messed with in the past. A great crowd, an absolutely perfect crowd, and it was our job to keep them happy and high.

Some of the night is forever lost to me, but amid memories of avid yells and piercing whistles I have a misty sense that I never played better. In the daze of light and sound, I became drenched in each brief embrace of the music as its storming pulse tore through me before casting itself over the room. For a brief moment, I rose above the stage to look down on my svelte, long-haired and not-yet balding self as I slayed the Hammond beast in front of me one conquering riff at a time. With an arsenal of tremolos, flatted fifths, crushed thirds, and rotating Leslie horns, I plunged into the great musical abyss to be ultimately rewarded by the sweetest of all gifts offered by the Blues gods—a moment of pure bliss. I lingered as long as I could—and then it was over. I blinked—and was mortal again.

The evening continued with uncounted free beers, congratulatory back slaps, and suggestive cheek kisses. And later, the grandest handshake of them all: "Good job," B.B. told me as he engulfed my hand in his sausage-sized fingers. I stood there attempting to mutter some form of appreciation as he moved on towards the tour bus where his beloved Lucille patiently waited to be driven to the next town. I finished out the night with friends and booze, enjoying the company of both, and yet occasionally slipping off to ponder what that singular and slightly terrifying moment of clarity had done to me. Would I ever know that feeling again? Should I ever try?

Weeks later I took a day away from my usual scene and went to lie on the sand at Mission Beach. I spread out my towel and soaked in the sun while pink-skinned tourists carefully worked their way along the crowded boardwalk behind me. I found myself watching a pair of cops on mountain bikes hassle some shirtless locals about their open containers when a voice next to me said, "Hey, buddy."

I squinted in the brightness to see a scrappy-haired man with cobra tats up his freckled arms and smoking a cheap-smelling cigarette. I prepared myself for the usual variation on "Could you spot me some change so I can catch the bus back to where my car broke down?" But instead, heard a very different question. "Didn't you play keyboards for the B.B. King show?" Before I could respond he continued, "Yea, I thought so. I'm the sound man who ran the mixing board that night."

Starting to recognize him, I said, "Right. You did a great job making us sound good. Thanks." He took a final, deep drag off his smoke before flicking the butt away, nodded his head, and said, "Well, it was pretty clever the way you guys landed that gig. By the way, did anyone give you a recording of your set?" This was before the days of cell phones and hand-held digital recorders, so having a decent recording of a live gig was a sought-after rarity and my answer would normally have been an interested "No," but I ignored the question.

I was much more intrigued by the flippant way he seemed to think I was in on some sort of deception. "What do you mean?" I asked. "We fought hard to earn that gig just like everyone else and came out on top." "Well I suppose," he replied, "but your manager offering to rent the Hammond, pay for its delivery and everything—saved the club a bundle. None of the other bands thought of that."

"You know," he continued, "I ran a mix of the whole show onto my personal recording deck. Would you like a copy so you can hear how you sounded that night?" I turned towards the surf line and noticed a young boy scrambling after a ball only to stumble to the sand as the steel-gray water eased up around his legs. His face looked perplexed as if he hadn't decided yet if the fall would make him cry or giggle. A woman rushed to pick him up, and seeing her he quickly made up his mind with a loud whine. I sucked in the brittle air and put my sunglasses on. "No thanks," I said.

CHAPTER 10: DREADLOCKS AND RECORD COMPANIES

"DUDE, DO YOU KNOW who that is?" asked my friend and roommate Mark, as we each enjoyed a pint at Monte's Pub on the campus of San Diego State University. I looked towards the direction of his gesture and saw a shirtless, strapping, young black man with a perfect head of dreadlocks as he drifted among the tables. With an unhurried stride, he politely handed out flyers and engaged in conversation with the other mid-afternoon imbibers. "No clue," I said, pushing aside the remnants of my second fish taco, "but I see the girls seem to like him." The man had the So-Cal-Reggae look nailed and at that moment, I found myself feeling downright envious.

He soon came by our table, the immediately likable Trevor James. The flyer he handed us promoted an upcoming gig for his self-named band. "You should come check us out, mon," he said with a nice Jamaican accent. I found out later he was from New York, but at the moment, I bought into the image he was selling. Mark and I, both being musicians, invited him to sit and tell us about his band. The three of us had an interesting conversation about how Trevor was being courted by several major record labels, and the gigs he did locally were just to keep sharp until he went national. Things got even more intriguing when he said he could use a second keyboardist if I was interested in auditioning.

Soon enough, I was the newest member of the Trevor James Band, and we had gigs all over San Diego County and beyond. Between my blues gigs, teaching piano lessons, and now the reggae scene, I was making a couple grand a month and feeling pretty badass about the whole "being a full-time musician" thing.

I lost track of how many gigs with Trevor seemed to just barely come together. I'd swear he would tell the whole band to show up at a bar that had no idea we were coming. Upon all of us bounding through the doors with equipment, the ever-cool Trevor would take the clueless manager aside for a brief conversation and just like that, the gig was on. If there was a documentary on guerilla booking tactics for musicians, Trevor would be the star.

One of our shows was booked for a big beach party event in Rosarito, Mexico, and because I had a hatchback that could seat four and fit some gear in the back, I ended being one of the drivers.

What I saw at the gig was years before the whole "Girls Gone Crazy" video craze, but could have easily served as the template. G-strings flossing, bikini tops dropping, tequila shots popping, and beer never stopping, while the reggae bands played on. That night, the band members, with an equal number of friendly girls we had met, all crammed into a bungalow for a sleepless evening as the party continued just outside.

The next day was a blur as we spent another afternoon performing and being entertained by the crowd. We weren't given accommodations for a second night, so several of us loaded up my car to head home and almost died a fiery death in the Baja desert.

Not being able to read the Spanish signs very well, and being ill-advised by my still-drunk passengers, I entered the wrong side of a one-way highway. All too soon, the headlights of an oncoming truck convinced me something was terribly wrong, and I dodged off the side of the road in the nick of time, scrapping a guard rail. Amazingly, the only casualty was the front bumper, which had to be removed and stowed before we soldiered on.

By the time we made it to the border check-point around dawn, we were a haggard crew, but I noticed that one of the band members had perked up and was suggesting the rest of us all act civil to the officials. Sure enough, a car full of reggae musicians, music equipment, and a torn bumper resulted in us being sent to the secondary inspection area for a comprehensive search.

It was a hassle to unload everything from the car only to reload it again, but soon we were on our way. Only when we had driven several miles up Interstate 5 into the U.S. did the "perky" one admit his instrument case was full of dope and had no idea how we passed inspection. I could have killed that guy, but I was too exhausted.

♦ ♦ ♦

True to Trevor's word, we were getting some buzz from Electra which was a major record company at the time. We partied with their production assistants at the home of an escort-service owner who made sure plenty of pretty girls were around to brighten up the scenery. They had already heard us before, but we played a few more songs for them pool-side, and they agreed to put the wheels in motion for us to get signed to a record deal.

In the meantime, we kept playing a few gigs around San Diego, and I didn't realize the relevance until much later, but I began noticing a few peculiar events. At one bar, the manager argued about letting us play because he'd been getting phone calls all day that people would boycott the place if we performed. Boycott? I had no idea why would anyone boycott a reggae band. At another gig, a young lady shouted, "You're going to get what you deserve Trevor," as she walked out the door. Lastly, Trevor showed up very late once for a rehearsal wearing slacks, a short-sleeved dress shirt, and narrow black tie—none of which fit him (literally or stylistically), suggesting he had borrowed the outfit. When I asked, "What's with the clothes?" he mumbled something about having to be in court but didn't elaborate. I let it go, figuring it was for jury duty or something.

Eventually, the date was set for our showcase performance at the renowned SIR Studios in Los Angeles. Our patrons catered the whole thing and put on a great spread to keep the invite-only guests happy. The producers from Electra were present and excited. This was it—our chance at the fabled major-label record deal! All that was needed was for us to play a solid set with our enigmatic lead singer and all would be well. But there was no Trevor. He never arrived. In fact, it would be years before he arrived anywhere except prison.

It took me weeks to finally gather all the information, but it seemed Trevor had a taste for young—very young—blond girls and didn't understand the concept of "No." Although there were several cases the police had become aware of, Trevor was convicted of sexual misbehavior against one girl on the very day of our showcase. He naively assumed he would be found innocent and make it up to L.A. in time for the gig. The entire time he was being tried, Trevor was able to keep it mostly under the radar. Only the lead guitarist knew what was up, and he blamed it on the "stupid bitches who set Trevor up."

Meanwhile, back at the showcase, we played a few songs on our own with one of the other bandmembers singing, but it was just to save face. We were toast, the producers weren't amused, and Electra would not be doling out any contracts that night.

Weeks later, I answered the phone to hear a lady's voice say, "Collect call from Trevor Johnson from the San Diego County Jail. Will you accept the charges?" I could hear Trevor loudly complaining about being misnamed a Johnson. In a flurry of unrehearsed frustration, all I could do was yell, "No I won't accept, and don't you ever call me again asshole!" Not too original, but it will have to stand as my final contact with Trevor.

ENDNOTE:

A couple decades after all these events, I got an email from someone claiming he was a 20-year-old child of Trevor James but didn't know anything about his father. He came across my name in an internet search because I had mentioned being a member of the band in an article on the web. He wanted to know what I could tell him about his father and if I could put him in touch.

I have to admit, I pulled my punches and simply told him Trevor was an excellent performer, but other projects came up and the band members all lost contact. The criminal-justice outcome of this chapter can be verified by a visit to the San Diego Courthouse, but I'm sure the story of what came before depends on who you ask.

I had some good times with the band, no doubt about it, but I think about the young girls who came under Trevor's sway, and I wish I had never had lunch in Monte's Pub that day he walked in.

Age 23 with the Trevor James Band (Trevor 2nd from right)

CHAPTER 11: SMOOTH JAZZ AND A SERIAL RAPIST

KIM CALDWELL MOVED ASIDE THE GREASY WRAPPERS which minutes earlier contained her late-night dinner from Taco Bell. It was two in the morning and time for her to finally go to bed. Her Pacific Beach apartment was noisy, like all beach apartments in that San Diego suburb, but she nodded off soon enough. In the dim world of half-sleep, there was a threatening sound coming from the window, a dark shadow where there should be none, and the sudden awareness that a hooded figure was coming for her.

The next hour was spent being raped at knifepoint by the man referred to locally as the "PB Rapist." Kim realized she was in the throes of becoming victim number seven to the serial assailant who had been in the headlines for several months. Although she keenly suffered the agony of each moment, Kim was able to accomplish something the first six had not—she saw opportunity to be the end of this man above her. She studied his eyes, his breathing, his speech, his carriage, and when finally free of his clutch, she treated her body as a crime scene not to be disturbed more than necessary. She would not become a number. She would become his ruin.

♦ ♦ ♦

San Diego in the early 1990s was at the center of a growing musical movement in the United States. Tired of making miserable wages in the usual downtown jazz holes, many of the area musicians began playing music that blended the jazz improvisation they loved with the sensibility of the soul and funk music they grew up with. Being more akin to instrumental pop music than traditional jazz, this new genre quickly sprouted a healthy following. Being a year-round destination for tourists and corporate events, San Diego was especially well-suited for the new "smooth" jazz. Soon, it seemed every hotel lounge, open-air shopping mall, city park, conference center ballroom, and upscale nightclub in the county featured live music sponsored by FM radio's "Light's Out" station, 92.7. Gigs were plentiful, and for most of the local performers embracing this new fusion it was the first time they were able to make good money playing music they could still consider jazz.

Vocalist Kenneth Bogard, known simply as "Bogie," saw the potential for combining the rhythms of reggae music with the refined qualities of smooth jazz and eventually created a unique style of music with his band, "Dr. Chico's Island Sounds." They became a San Diego mainstay and worked solidly every week. I saw them several times at some of the nicest venues in town, and being a musician primarily involved with the local blues scene, envied their popularity and remuneration.

At the height of Dr. Chico's popularity, I got an unexpected phone call from their singer after he tracked down my number from a mutual friend. "Eh mon, my name is Bogie and I need a keyboardist for a few gigs. Are you interested?" Not hearing an immediate response from me, Bogie continued, "My regular guy needs a couple weeks off for medical reasons so we need a sub for some gigs in Mission Valley." If I could land the gig with Island Sounds, even temporarily, my credibility among musicians in town would quickly rise, so I tried to answer in a tone that sounded interested but not desperate. "Sounds fun."

A couple days later, Bogie showed up at my place with a guitar case slung over his shoulder and holding a small amp. He wore a headband that highlighted his short but spikey blond hair (think lead vocalist of Loverboy singing "Everybody's workin' for the weekend"). His grin of slightly crooked teeth bordered on dopey, but my first impression was to like the guy. I already respected him as a musician and was quickly drawn to his laid-back style, so what was not to like? We set up in my bedroom and played through a few tunes from his usual setlist. My ego would love to recall how we easily blended our styles and knew within the first chorus we had found a long-lost musical brother, but it just didn't happen. The syncopation he was used to just didn't feel natural to me. I plodded roughly through our first rehearsal and within fifteen minutes knew there would not be a second. I started looking around the room pondering how to extract myself from the situation and was moments away from feigning excruciating gas pains when, in a moment of blissful co-understanding, Bogie asked, "You like Thai food?" Within minutes our gear was packed and we were headed over to the Copper Dragon on University Avenue.

"You've got to try the lemon-grass chicken. It's wicked good." I took Bogie's suggestion and also ordered a pot of green tea for us to share. This was working out after all. Even if we weren't to become serious musical partners, at least we could cross paths in the future with no awkward moments pretending not to see each other. As he hungrily cut into his breast meat, we chatted about the local music scene and he referred me to a percussionist friend named Biter who was looking for a keyboardist. After enjoying the rest of our conversation and meal, I took a final sip from the tea cup, and we rose to say our goodbyes. He picked up the tab and I laid down a tip. We waved goodbye with him pulling away in an undistinguished sedan and me on my Yamaha. Except for some upcoming appearances on local television, I never saw the man again.

♦ ♦ ♦

San Diego State University, usually called "State" by its 35,000 students, was one hell of a fun school back then. Playboy magazine rated it as the third-best party school in the nation which quickly gave rise to t-shirts and bumper stickers proclaiming, "#3 and Improving." The riotous student life necessitated an active University police force that spent considerable hours patrolling the neighborhood parties, sometimes attended by hundreds. The school cops were specifically on the hunt for a flasher who had been accosting females as they left parties alone. He had been nick-named "Zorro" due to the Lone Ranger-style mask used to cover his face. Eventually, one of these women thought she recognized Zorro as a popular San Diego singer, but without more evidence the campus police could only watch and wait for the man they now suspected was Kenneth Bogard to make a mistake as the masked flasher.

Meanwhile, an eighth attack was in the news. The PB Rapist struck again except, instead of his usual ski mask, this time he wore a Zorro mask. At first the city police thought it might have been an inaccurate copy-cat, but the SDSU cops thought differently and turned over a name from their pervert files. Using a ruse, San Diego police convinced Bogard to provide a saliva swab to clear him in a case he knew he had nothing to do with. Still a new forensic tool at the time, Bogie had not considered that one of his victims had the presence of mind to collect his DNA after he raped and terrified her.

"Son of a BITCH," I said out loud when I saw the news on TV how the police had arrested their number one suspect—the same guy I had shared a pleasant meal with only a month before. Eventually, Kim Caldwell's evidence and brutally accurate court testimony was convincing enough to gain not only a guilty verdict on 36 charges but a 96-year sentence for the PB Rapist, Kenneth Bogard.

About a year after the conviction I picked up Biter so we could share a ride to a gig playing in a musical theater pit band. I had followed up on Bogie's recommendation, and Biter and I had played several gigs together before this one came along. As we drove south on I-805 towards Chula Vista, I turned on the radio to hear the top-of-the-hour local news. The announcer commented how Kim Caldwell was continuing the fight for rape-victim advocacy. During the PB Rapist case she had fought hard to embarrass the city into creating a rape task force and now she was using her clout to further the rights of women often too afraid to speak out for themselves. I was thinking to myself, "That woman is awesome," and was about to verbalize my thoughts when Biter vehemently interjected, "Fucking Kim Caldwell! I wish that bitch would just shut up and go away. I can't believe what she's done to Bogie." I asked him to explain how any of this wasn't Bogie's own fault, but his response was only hate-filled muttering. That was the last gig ever I played with Biter.

As for Bogie, after two failed appeal attempts, he will be in his eighties before he can be considered for parole.

ENDNOTE:

Earlier versions of this chapter were originally posted on a blog several years ago. Since all the events happened pre-internet, there isn't much information about the PB Rapist online, so a Google search leads to my article, and several people have reached out to me. Most of the responses fall into the category of, "I use to know/date/perform with Bogie; he was nice to me, but what a creep he turned out to be." Two of the responders, however, truly caught me off guard.

Kim Caldwell herself reached out to let me know she appreciated how I presented the events, and that I got most of the details right. In our follow up emails, she expressed some interest in sharing more of her story now that she can look back on it with some distance, but she wasn't sure yet. A few years later, in the summer of 2018, I was contacted by the producers of a true-crime TV show hosted by Paula Zahn to see if I could encourage Kim to revisit the story for broadcast. She didn't return my emails, so I guess she's still not ready. I don't blame her.

Even more surprisingly, I heard from Bogie himself, although indirectly. A previous acquaintance of the rapist wanted to share some of his thoughts about the case and we met for lunch, at which time he gave me photocopies of several letters Bogie had written from behind bars during the timeframe of his trial and early incarceration.

They were fascinating. Childishly naïve and dripping with glorious declarations of God-endorsed innocence; they paint a picture of a scared and desperate convict. He was certain that a jailhouse assassination was imminent, and he needed to prove they got the wrong man before it was too late. Neither event ever took place.

Shortly before Bogie was arrested, he gave an interview regarding his music career in which he eerily declared his dream to become famous: "I want to be internationally known...I want the whole world to know who I am, to know my name."

For the wrong reasons, perhaps Bogie got some of what he wanted...but after decades in prison with no release in sight, surely, he also got what he deserved.

CHAPTER 12: GEORGE BENSON MUST THINK I'M AN IDIOT

OVER THE YEARS, I'VE GATHERED a few fancy pieces of paper that hang on my wall and purport knowledge gained. I don't dispute that I learned a few things in the hallowed halls of academia, but I had another school just as important. For a while in the early 1990s, I got to study at the feet of a guitarist/vocalist named Billy Thompson and class met anywhere and anytime he let me hang out with him.

Billy (BT in my mind) was the leader of the Mighty Penguins that were regarded as the top-flight blues act in San Diego, but they hadn't been working much at the time due to some internal differences. For reasons I've never understood but always appreciated, BT took to me and let me play in his pick-up bands for several months while he was trying out some new ideas and deciding what direction to take his material.

Getting to jam with him night after night, and hearing his blistering explorations and rhythmic ferociousness was sometimes overwhelming. He would wrap up another of his seemingly effortless, bad-ass solos and give me the nod to go next, and I'd think, "You've got to be kidding me!" But I hung in there, studied the homework he implied, and kept coming back to the classes he held for me in the various bars and juke-joints we performed in.

One of the most important things BT ever taught me was to not get caught up trying to be the baddest cat in town. He said, "Man, I don't give a rip if somebody says I'm the guitarist to beat around here. I only compare myself to my heroes, not some fool in a local beach bar." That one has stayed with me every day of my life for decades now. Any time I get complacent, start to get soft, or stop pushing myself to improve as a man or musician, I take heed of BT's lesson. As soon as I feel like I'm becoming the big fish, it's time to move my tail to a bigger pond.

My esteem for BT as a mentor is all the more poignant when I recall the unfortunate afternoon when it was me who became the fool at a local restaurant-bar. Elario's Bistro Sky-Lounge was an elegant dinner-showroom on the top floor of a hotel overlooking the beach in La Jolla, California, and BT had a steady gig there, not as a performer, but as production manager and soundman.

As another component of BT's tutelage, he called me one day and said, "Hey Bud, I need to get the piano dialed in for an act tonight. Come on down to the club and bang on the keys while I move the microphones around." Always eager to help the man, I obliged and soon found myself entering the main dining room to be awestruck by the gorgeous view that day: crystal blue waters under a tangerine sky.

I proceeded past the bar and noticed a well-groomed man seated by himself sipping a cocktail. The bar didn't officially open until closer to dinner so I noted that he must be a high-rolling businessman for the management to accommodate an afternoon drinker. I moved on towards the stage and took a seat at the baby grand. "Ready when you are BT," I announced. "Sweet," he responded. "Just play anything for a while and I'll try some different settings."

It's not unusual for musicians to fall into rituals when preparing to perform. After putting on new strings, many guitarists will go straight to an open D chord to check the tuning. Singers might repeat a favorite catch phrase or melodic fragment when checking microphones. And drummers often have an elaborate series of warm-ups they play while tuning their drums to the room.

Somewhere along my musical journey, I acquired the habit of getting familiar with a new room or piano by playing the opening two chords that were popular in the smooth-jazz hit, "This Masquerade." Musicians know these chords as F minor 9th followed by B-flat 13th. I sat there and began my ritual like I had so many times before without any hesitation. BT immediately gave me a questioning raised eyebrow, but I figured he was just dismayed by the frequencies coming through the sound system and I continued to plod ahead with my warm-up chords for the next several minutes.

Finally, BT got the microphones set in a position he found pleasing and said, "Okay, that's enough. Come on down from the stage." I approached him thinking I might hear some words of appreciation, but instead BT asked, "So you think you're gonna get a gig or something doing that?" "What you talkin' about Billy? I was just jamming so you could get a sound check." "Dude," he exclaimed, "That's George Benson sitting at the bar: the guy who made 'This Masquerade' famous, and you just spent the last few minutes stickin' it in his face!"

The words were like a punch to the gut. I was horrified at the thought that I had just spent all that time inadvertently saying to the great guitarist-vocalist, "Look at me, look at me," like some annoying local hack. Now, if this were a 1940's Hollywood movie, Benson would have come over to me and said, "Kid, you've got moxie and I like your style. It just so happens I need a new pianist, so give me a call."

Well, he did eventually saunter over, but only to talk with BT. Earlier in his career, Benson played Elario's and remembered the incredible view, so while he had some time to kill before his show that night at a larger venue, he came by for a drink. He and BT were soon chatting it up like old friends, and doing what guitarists always inevitably do—talk about gear. Meanwhile, I disappeared into the corner and kept my mouth shut.

Later, when BT and I were alone, I asked, "Benson didn't say anything about my silliness on the piano did he?" "Nope," he answered. "Never came up." I was immensely relieved and yet slightly disappointed at the same time. Pride and vanity often get blurry in my musician brain.

In the months and years to come, BT and I slowly drifted apart, though there was no malice or disagreement. He had other opportunities, and I moved away from blues towards genres that tended to pay better. These days he's tearing it up along the east coast still making great music. George Benson has continued on to be a legendary figure in jazz and popular music. And me, well, I still warm up with those same two chords and chuckle at myself while I'm doin' it.

CHAPTER 13: SHOW TUNES AND LIPSTICK LESBIANS

EVERY THURSDAY IN SAN DIEGO was when the weekly *Reader* news and entertainment paper was published. Back around 1990 there were three sections in each edition but as a musician, I was usually most interested in the classified ads. This was where pre-internet musicians got their gossip and looked for deals. What drummer finally got caught dating the guitarist's girlfriend, forcing a band to advertise for a new member? What locally owned music store had lowered the price of that Mexican-made electric bass yet again? What saxophonist placed a "Reward" notice after he was too stoned to remember leaving his horn on the curb after a gig in the Gaslamp District?

My ad was there every week too. "Modern Keyboard Studies" was the headline. It went on to promise certain advancement at a fair rate: $30 for each hour-long lesson. I usually never had more than a dozen students at a time, but the ad always turned a profit so I just let it run.

Most of the calls I received went like this:

Caller: Hi. Um, how many lessons until I'm good?

Me: Six months to a year. [I had learned long before that no one wanted the truth that it would be somewhere between years and never.]

Caller: Um, okay. Is the first lesson free?

Me: No. I provide a quality product and it has a value. [My main competitor in town had been doing the "Free First Lesson" thing for years, so I embraced the tactic that I was above such a desperate plea for new business—it didn't always work, but at least I never wasted my time with one-lesson bargain hunters.]

Caller: Um, when can I start?

Ka-ching! But not all callers stayed on the script. There was the woman who said she had two-inch fingernails that she was not willing to trim and asked, "Will that be a problem when I play?" I referred her to the freebie guy.

And then there was the man who said he wanted to schedule two hours a week but informed me he would never actually show up. When I pushed for an explanation he said, "Well, I need a cover story so my wife doesn't know I'm seeing someone on the side." Classy. I passed, and he mumbled something about not going to yoga instead.

But a phone call that had a profound effect on my life came from one John Van Dyke. Unlike most of the inquiries I got from the ad, he wasn't calling about lessons; he was a singer in need of a keyboardist for a gig starting the very next week. John optimistically asked, "Maybe you have a student who's ready to start gigging?" Always looking for more paying jobs, I replied, "Well, tell me more. Maybe I'd be interested myself."

John went on to describe a pretty sweet gig: four weekends of work at a local club that paid $100 per night playing a combination of show tunes, jazz standards, pop ballads, and a smattering of R & B. I remember thinking, "I've played a lot around town and I can't think of any place that pays that well for that kind of setlist." Then it finally came out—it was a gay bar. "That explains why I've never heard of it," said my under-enlightened and heterosexual self. It only took a moment for me to reflect that as a full-time musician I was at all times subservient to one maxim: No Gig—No Eat.

"I'll do it!" I declared.

The band was typical for the cabarets of the day: I played all the accompaniment myself with left-hand bass lines and right-hand chords while a drum machine kept the beat. We were joined by a second singer: the tall, dark, and handsome Andy Anderson; and a saxophonist: the tall, talented, and not-so-dark Don Bowman. The act was thrown together pretty quick, but we came up with just enough music for the opening night, knowing we'd have to add more material in the following days.

So, there I was, all dressed up in my hopelessly hetero clothes having a drink before the show, looking around the room with wide-eyed wonder. I noticed some very rugged ladies at the end of the bar and Andy grinned.

"Straight guys crack me up!" he said. "You all just fantasize about lipstick lesbians." I had no idea what he that meant, but he had my attention.

"Well, on behalf of straight guys everywhere, I'll bite."

I knocked back the rest of my tequila shot, sucked in some air between my teeth as the liquid hit the back of my throat, and tossed him a slow pitch right over the plate.

"Okay Andy! What's a lipstick lesbian?"

"Well, funny you ask Mister Girl!" he said with a full-voiced laugh at the new nickname just bestowed upon me. He and his gay friends often called each other "gurrrrl," but for me he graciously added the "Mister."

"They're gorgeous Penthouse-type models that in all ways look totally hot for straight men in their high heels and makeup but have a thing for women at the same time."

"Ah yes, I see" I said as I surveyed the rest of the crowded club. "So, when do they get here?"

"Keep dreaming," said Andy. "Come on, show time. Let's give the people what they want."

And we did—not only that night but many days and nights for the next several years. We added a soulful, female singer named Corliss, and calling ourselves "Impromptu," played what seemed like every gay bar in southern California. The Escape, the Loft, W.D.'s, Bourbon Street, Ripples, and a long-standing run at the Little Shrimp in Laguna Beach: we hit them all.

I must say, the gay-bar scene was a great education for me. I made some excellent friends, learned a lot of great songs, earned good money, picked up several private party gigs at beautiful southern

California estates, and met some lovely straight women (the girls hanging out with their gay man-friends found me rather enigmatic as the only one in the room whose flirts had any bite).

And while out among the patrons of those many interesting places during those many interesting times, I witnessed extremes of sophistication, depravity, humor, tragedy, love, sadness, and hope: but Penthouse-model lesbians with lipstick? —Not so much.

Age 25 with "Impromptu"

CHAPTER 14: ALL GIGS END

I PUT DOWN MY THIRD BEER and adjusted the guitar in my lap before beginning another song.

"In...my loneliness,
When you've gone and I'm all by myself
And I need your caress."

Gabby's full-grown Siberian husky, locked in a nearby pen, pranced and whined at my poor imitation of Bossa Nova crooning. I ignored the criticism and sang on.

I had told Gabby I'd be at his house by 4:30 p.m. but after no one answered the door, I found the open gate to his backyard where I kicked back on the patio furniture and pulled out my Korean-made acoustic guitar. Although proficient on the keyboard, I had only been playing guitar about a year and brought it with me to try out some old jazz standards with my vocalist friend. After tuning up, I began feeling the late-afternoon heat of the Chino Hills sun on my head and remembered he had an outdoor bar-b-que with a built-in refrigerator. "What are the chances?" I pondered as I opened a small stainless-steel door under the grill. "Yes!" I said aloud and pulled out a first can of crappy but cold domestic. An hour later and well lubricated, I proudly concluded my Brazilian serenade to the captive canine audience:

"I... will wait for you,
Meditating how sweet life can be
When you come back to me"

Finally succumbing to the heat and alcohol, I slid further into the chair's sagging, plastic straps and nodded off to dream of fruity cocktails and sandy beaches.

The acrid odor of cigar smoke slapped me awake. It was now evening and an amber porch light provided a soft glow. Gabby sat next to me with a smoldering Macanudo between his fingers. "Good to see you, Doogie," he said with a chuckle, knowing I tolerated that nickname only from him. "Sorry about being so late, but things got pretty messy at work. One of the clients wouldn't stop bashing his head into the bed rail and it took me a long time to get a helmet on him and write up the paperwork. Crazy fuck almost bit me."

⬧ ⬧ ⬧

Gabby had begun working with the mentally and physically disabled not long after our band "Joe Cool and the Rumblers" had broken up for good. I was the first rat to leave that ship. Previously, it had been easy for me to leave a band since I had trained myself to feel little allegiance to the many I had been in. A bandleader would call me up, give me the details, and if I was free, I took the job. I'd show up in my generic black suit, play tunes from the same setlist every other cover band in town drew from, shake hands at the end of the night when I got paid, and move on. Maybe I'd work with that band again, maybe not. I didn't care much either way as long as the check cleared. But the Rumblers were different. Their members were old-school and leaving that band was complicated. Getting in the band hadn't been easy either.

Several years earlier I responded to a classified ad in the San Diego Reader soliciting a keyboardist for a "popular, working, southern California oldies band." For quite some time I had been playing the gay bar circuit (The Escape, Briefs, The Little Shrimp, Ripples, etc.); plenty of work for a keyboardist who could play left-hand bass and work a drum machine, but the novelty of being the only straight guy in a room full of svelte fellows and swarthy gals had worn off. Anxious for new opportunities, I scheduled an audition and drove up to Pomona to meet the members of the band I had heard of many times but never seen perform. I had to admit they were playing gigs above my current station—nicer venues, better pay, and connections with booking agents who, to that point, wouldn't return my phone calls. I wanted a taste of their success and arrived ready to play my best stuff on the agreed-to songs.

As I was setting up my rig, I asked why they needed a new keyboardist and heard guarded answers about how the previous guy had been spending too much off-time drinking his pay at the beach bars in Orange County. After a quick sound check we ran through "My Girl," "Great Balls 'O Fire," and "Runaway," before I was told, "Give us a minute, we wanna talk." Stepping outside, I knelt down to play with a young pup I found penned across the walkway. Being drawn to its one white eye and happy little face, I said, "Here's the deal...if they offer me the position, I won't say the first thing that comes to mind 'cause it'll probably be some sarcastic shit that gets me in trouble. I'll take a moment and say the *second* thing that comes to mind. Sound like a good plan?" Although it was probably just a request for more attention, I accepted the playful nip on my fingers as confirmation.

A few minutes later I was summoned back to the rehearsal room and asked by the lead singer, "How would you get out of the other gigs you have now if we offered you the spot?" I immediately responded, "Well, Gabriel, I'll refer them to a drunk-ass, has-been down in Laguna Beach looking for work." Doh! Realizing too late I had most-certainly just insulted their fallen brother-in-arms, a moment of awkward silence fell over the room, and I prepared to hear the polite but obvious, "We'll let you know." Much to my surprise, the room erupted in laughter, and I heard, "We think you'll fit in just fine, and call me Gabby."

Although they were an odd lot to be around, I learned a lot from those guys over the next couple of years. Girlfriends are expendable, wives might come and go, grown offspring may want nothing to do with you, but NO ONE QUITS THE BAND. You might get forced out, but you don't quit. The drummer, bassist, and guitarist had been playing together for twenty-five years. Two of them hadn't spoken directly to each other in over a decade. So what? —You don't quit the band. One of them slept with another's not-yet ex-wife while they were separated. Get over it—you don't quit the band.

With well over twenty years of singing, this was still only Gabby's second band so even though the Rumblers still considered him a new guy after a mere eight years of membership, he fit well into the group's philosophy. They probably suspected letting a young gun like me into their coven was the beginning of the end—and rightly so. I was part of the newer generation of working musicians who, as a matter of survival, purposely avoided overly committing to any one project and although I admired the hell out of their loyalty, I considered it quaint and didn't really get it.

During my two years with the band, we played some pretty sweet gigs: several days at the California State Fair; an end-of-season wrap party for the cast of "Beverly Hills 90210"; a few nights backing Bowser from the old Sha-Na-Na group; traveling all over the southwest providing entertainment for a crafts fair; oldies nights at a popular amusement park; some great nightclubs; and more wedding receptions and corporate parties than I can remember.

I was thoroughly impressed at how seriously the group took their work. We always arrived at a venue at least a few hours ahead of the downbeat. Plenty of time was allotted to a sound check to make sure we could all hear well. The client was always treated with respect, regardless of how big of a prick he (or she) was, and we refused to work for less than $1,250 which was split evenly—if the money got funny, we hit the road. It was a major turning point in my career to learn that no matter what kind of music I created, I didn't have to accept mediocrity from myself, the musicians on-stage with me, or the people writing the checks. We provided a rock-solid, consistently professional product, and we deserved to be treated well and paid on time. Many musicians I previously worked with had not yet developed that creed. But even good gigs and steady pay couldn't keep me from admitting I had a growing problem being in the band.

During a week-long November engagement in Las Vegas, Bill Clinton was elected to his first term as commander-in-chief, and it really freaked me out that for the first time, I was in a rock band with members older than the president. At the hotel bar I listened to the guys talk at length about "the old days" and how their young adulthood seemed to flash by. I looked into their mid-life-crisis faces and in a jolt of reality saw my future. In the blink of an unwary eye, I would be in my late forties playing the same old songs in exactly the same order in the same key with the same solos and the same endings and the same scripted "spontaneous" banter until the day I mercifully died pounding out those same damn redundant chords in "At the Hop."

Gabby and I often drove together when we played out of town, and on our way back from Vegas he picked up on my vibe and said, "You got something on your mind, Chief?" After a pensive breath I answered, "Gab, you and I have become good friends, and I don't mean to put you down, but here's the truth...I don't want to become you. I mean, you've been playing exactly the same shit for years now and if you're cool with it, then more power to ya, but I'm about to put a bullet through my head just thinking about doing this when I'm your age."

Gabby snuffed out a cigarette in the truck's ashtray and coolly responded, "Doogie, if you're still doing this at my age, *I'm* the one who will put a bullet in your head. I would like nothing better than to pick you up for a gig someday to hear you say, 'Keep on driving, I'm done.' God knows I've been having similar thoughts about wanting out, but it's different for me. I may not be able to break away, but you, you little son-of-a-bitch, quit jerkin' off with us and go do something with your life while you can." On the radio we heard the opening bass riff to Zeppelin's "How Many More Times," and he kicked up the volume. Taking the hint this conversation was over, I turned towards the passenger-side window and counted the Joshua trees on the horizon.

A couple months later I got word the band was offered two weeks work in a mud-scrape of a small town in northern Nevada. Apparently, a mining company ran the only bar in the area and used it to make back the wages paid out to employees who had nowhere else to go after work. It would be the band's job to keep them entertained and buying drinks for the ladies (also provided by the management). "No thanks," I told the bass player after he tried to convince me it was a worthwhile gig. "I think it's time for me to cut bait, and you can work in somebody new while you're holed-up there." I knew this was the right decision, but for the first time in years I felt bad, even disloyal, leaving a band. To soften the blow and ease my guilt, I wrote up a book of chord charts so the next keyboardist would have an easier time learning the set. I handed over the music, accepted my last check, and formally ended my days as a Rumbler.

More surprising than my own defection was that Gabby soon followed my lead and quit the group. He saw the writing on the wall for an aging oldies band. The quality gigs were drying up, and Gabby knew it would only be a matter of time before he couldn't support his family. The trigger had to be pulled before the band faced its inevitable slow death. The other members had found my parting inconvenient, but not much of a shock, and they replaced me soon enough. But with Gabby's exit, the group imploded. A member of their inner-circle had done the unthinkable and actually quit the band. One of southern California's premier oldies bands was in tatters and the members all staggered away to start new careers.

In a further act of courage, Gabby went to an occupational training center with only his high school diploma and army discharge papers to show for a lifelong dedication to music, and he plainly stated, "I'm forty-eight. I want to work. What can I do?"

♦ ♦ ♦

"Crazy fuck almost bit me," Gabby said as he handed me a lighter in the pleasant evening air on his patio. We spent the next couple hours drinking, smoking, and playing old tunes from the likes of Johnny Mercer, Cole Porter, and Carlos Jobim. Gabby's singing voice was a little rusty, but there was still ample evidence of his once audience-gripping pipes.

I was moved to joy getting to hear his delicate phrasing of those classic, silky lyrics, and at one point thanked him for making time to hang out. After a thoughtful moment he said, "Doogie, when I quit singing in the Rumblers I decided to quit singing, period. My time as a vocalist is over. I'm moving on. When you asked to come over today, I told myself this would be it. I won't sing again after tonight."

For guys like him, quitting the band was only possible if he walked away from all of it. That was the deal he made at the crossroads, and the transaction was about to be completed. After a while I once again strummed the plaintive chords to "Meditation" and swallowed hard when my friend sang the last line:

"I...will wait for you,
Meditating how sweet life can be
When you come back to me"

Gabby was good to his word. When his mother passed away and family assumed he would sing at the service, "No," he said, "I don't sing anymore." His youngest daughter was proposed to and hoped he would sing for her wedding day. "No, Sweetie," he said, "I'm not a singer anymore." Eventually, the original members of the Rumblers asked to re-unite for a one-time show just for family too young to have heard them perform and old friends wanting one more trip to the well. "No," he calmly answered, "No more."

When we visited each other years later, I finished sharing some of my recent music exploits and couldn't help but ask him, "Gabby, do you miss it?" As he took a moment to respond I noticed the passing of years on his body: the smattering of white in his once-envied dark mane; omnipresent eyeglasses, previously only used for reading; and twenty extra pounds as the price to pay for quitting cigarettes cold turkey. "Listen, man," he said leaning in closely, "all gigs end and that's a fact. All I did was choose the place and time."

I was wrong about what I had told him years earlier. When the lights dim on my swan song, becoming more like Gabby will be just fine.

Age 26 with the Rumblers

CHAPTER 15: THE CHURCH GIG

MY GOOD FRIEND AND MUSIC PARTNER at the time, Janet, called one day in the mid-1990s to say she might have a couple weeks of work at a church she often sang for. I have never been a church-going individual, but a gig is a gig. Over the next month, the questions put to me from the Minister progressed something like this:

"Would you be willing to play for us for a week or two until our regular pianist returns?"

A week later: "Would you be willing to finish out the month until our regular pianist returns?"

A couple weeks later: "Would you be willing to play through the holidays until our regular pianist returns?"

Five years later, I was still there and the other guy never returned.

The "other guy" was Nathan, one of the most stunningly talented musicians I've ever known. He is capable of hearing incredibly complex music ideas in his head and immediately translating them to two-handed passages on the keyboard or soaring melodies in his voice. These days, Nathan is still making great music with Janet and others around San Diego, but back in the mid-1990s he was not always able to follow through on gigs he accepted and this often resulted in me picking up last-minute work. I lost track of all the calls I got saying something like, "I booked Nathan, but he can't make it—can you be here in an hour?" I sometimes felt like a circling vulture waiting to swoop in on his kill, but he knew I was never purposely trying to take his gigs, and we always got along well.

If I was to ever attend a church regularly, a Unity denomination would be the closest fit for me, so I found myself comfortably sliding into my new job as "Music Director" at what was one of the larger Unity churches in the country. At the apex of my time there, we would see 1,200 people in attendance on a Sunday, spread over two services. Easter and Christmas Eve would bring in about 2,000.

This meant that no matter what kind of other gigs I might have had going on, I was guaranteed to perform in front of well over a thousand people every week! That was some substantial exposure, and I took it very seriously that so many people were counting on me to deliver a spiritually satisfying musical experience. In fact, it never failed that one or several people would compliment me on Sundays by saying, "You get better every week." The running joke among the other church musicians was, "Wow, you must have really sucked when you first got here." Indeed.

The process of creating the music for every Sunday went like this:

Mondays: research songs. This was pre-YouTube days so finding songs was an ongoing challenge. Each service required an opening "call to worship" song, two devotional group sing-alongs, two "pop" songs (one upbeat and one slow), and a closing "everything is awesome" group song. The non-pop songs were usually easier to program because they came from my archives and could be recycled. But the two pop songs were tough to find every week because they had to somehow support the theme of the message being presented by the minister. I used to rejoice when new Disney animated movies came out because that meant there would be an entire soundtrack of feel-good songs available to pillage.

Tuesdays: meet with the minister. We'd go over notes about recent music choices and performances, talk about upcoming topics she wanted the music to reinforce, and evaluate how our featured singers were performing. I'd also spend more time that day selecting music for upcoming services.

Wednesdays: I would create backing tracks in my home studio for the service to be held a week and a half later. The tracks for the immediate Sunday were already made the previous week. I created the tracks in my computer using various synthesizers and sound modules to emulate the existing recordings as closely as possible. Then I'd transpose everything to a key that would fit the singer assigned to that song, and then add some guitar parts and maybe even background vocals. The end result got mixed down to CD-R or cassette and delivered to the singer about a week ahead of time to begin practicing.

Thursdays: finish up the backing tracks from the previous day as needed. Rehearse with the singer for the Sunday coming up and hope that they had actually been practicing the material I gave them several days before.

Fridays: complete any of the tasks that never got done Monday through Thursday. Friday nights would often be filled with a performance gig.

Saturdays: put out fires when a singer is sick, lost their rehearsal tracks, or didn't really learn a song and wanted to do something else at the last minute. Saturday night I usually had a gig and sometimes that meant getting home after midnight and still having to unload my gear and spend a little time unwinding before bed.

Sunday mornings: wake up without nearly enough sleep and drag myself to church. Do a run-through with the singer and sound tech, and hope the minister didn't have a previously unmentioned problem with any of the music programmed for the day. Then we performed two services and made the magic happen.

Sunday afternoons: thank several people for saying I got even better that week, and then it was off to the In 'n' Out drive-thru for a burger and fries to take home in time to watch some football on TV. Then I spent the evening without thinking about the church gig for a whole 12 hours because come Monday, it started all over again.

In exchange for that relentless cycle of research-create-rehearse-perform, I was paid $1,500 per month by the time I left the job in the summer of 2000.

In all the time I was employed by the church, I always found it odd that I was never asked one obvious question by the staff or congregation: "Do you believe?" Instead, we engaged in a comfortable arrangement of non-communication on the subject. I provided top-quality music every week that aided in keeping bodies in the pews, and they paid me fairly for the work I did. I guess the deal was acceptable to both sides. They didn't ask, and I didn't tell.

Monetarily speaking, I was at the height of my San Diego-based career at this point. With teaching private lessons, working as a college adjunct, performing high-dollar gigs (I seldom worked for under $300 anymore), home-studio work, and the church gig, I pulled in over $45,000 a year and was by all local measurement a successful full-time musician.

Which could only mean one thing—it was time to move on.

CHAPTER 16: THAT'S *DOCTOR* BUTTHEAD TO YOU

SAN DIEGO STATE UNIVERSITY had a strong music department in the late 1990s. In particular, the Jazz Department, headed by Bill Yeager and Rick Helzer, was well regarded, and in 1998 I came knocking on doors to see who would let me in to earn a Master's Degree in Jazz Performance.

The problem from their perspective was, my SDSU undergraduate degree earned in 1989 was in psychology, not music. Rick knew what kind of pianist I was and wanted me to start right away, but the gatekeeper professors of music history and theory needed to be convinced. As a solution, my first semester was spent taking non-graduate classes through the community enrollment program instead of as a matriculated student. I aced the classes and was soon in the formal graduate program.

But the lesson I learned from this is that colleges are in no way motivated to graduate their students in a timely fashion. Head count is their bread and butter. They could have just let me start the regular program and flunk out if I wasn't up to it, but instead, they stretched out the process and ultimately kept me around for an extra semester. Because I didn't know how the game was played, I lost half a year off the front end of my eventual career as a professor.

What a difference it was to be taking college classes in my late 30s instead of age 22. Now, I sat in the front row (mostly because my vision and hearing had taken a beating over the years), asked questions constantly, had all my homework done early, read ahead in the coursework, and generally acted like Harry Potter's Herminie before she existed. And I loved every minute of it. I thrived on the subject matter and was growing exponentially as a musician, especially as a jazz pianist.

The graduate recital I presented was one of the high points of my musical life. The music I programmed was mostly from the traditional jazz idiom (Thelonious Monk, Bud Powell, Jimmy Smith), but I was allowed to bring in my own eclectic tastes with selections from Jeff Beck, Bjork, and Jane Siberry.

I put together a fabulous band comprised of other students and brought in my trusted singer-partner Janet Hammer to add some polish. The theater was completely packed with my friends, parents, other students, and supporters from my church gig. We played great, the house exploded in applause, and I held a catered reception afterwards—a real classy affair.

With my new graduate degree in hand, I soon found myself teaching adjunct at two community colleges in the San Diego area. I quickly learned that within academia the professors are placed into subcategories based on the emphasis of their graduate program. Even though I had more than enough knowledge to teach a section of Music Theory for example, that wasn't a class normally allotted to a "jazz guy." I was relegated to teaching either Jazz History or perhaps piano classes, and that was about it. For better or worse, the jazz-guy label would stay with me the entirety of my academic career, and that's something they don't explain when you pick your college major early in life.

On the plus side, I was at the pinnacle of my abilities as a jazz pianist during this timeframe. Fortunately, much of that skill-set was captured on a CD I made with Janet for which I wrote all the arrangements, hired the musicians, and directed the recording session.

She released the album under her own name as Never Let Me Go, and I'm quite proud of the music we created. The recording of the title track is particularly memorable to me. It features only piano and vocals, so the other musicians had left by this point. The lights had been dimmed in the studio, and we decided to let ourselves takes some risks and see how far we could extemporize on the original form. We did two complete takes and wholly poured ourselves into them. The juxtaposition of the lyrics against my piano accompaniment is striking. As Janet plaintively calls out for her lover to "never let go," I am simultaneously breaking like waves against convention while seeking new birth and transition.

That was the last time we ever recorded together, and the beginning of our movement towards less dependence upon each other after many years of being friends, lovers, and musical partners.

♦ ♦ ♦

After teaching a few college classes, I learned something wonderful about myself—I absolutely *loved* being in the classroom, and I wanted more. The drawback is that the most-desired positions as full-time, tenure-track music professors are reserved for those with doctorate degrees.

I soon learned that jazz doctorate programs had more than enough applicants and could be extremely selective. I first applied to the University of Southern California where I had previously met the Jazz Director various times and auditioned with him personally—rejected. Next up, the new and incredibly competitive jazz-composition program at the University of Miami—rejected. For my third attempt, the less competitive but still attractive program at the University of Texas-Austin—rejected.

So much for thinking this would be easy. I needed some guidance, and the Jazz Director at SDSU kindly put in a good word for me at the University of Northern Colorado in Greeley where there was an excellent secondary program in jazz pedagogy—accepted!

After 18 years in San Diego and succeeding as a full-time cover-band/country/blues/reggae/jazz/rock/pop/church/show-tune keyboardist, it was time to load up the rental truck and head across the Rocky Mountains. As an added bonus, my Dad made the drive with me, and we had a special time on the road together. He had lived in Colorado as a young man, and it was great hearing him talk about those days.

Two years, four months, and three weeks later (this time I knew how to play the game and finish on *my* schedule), I completed my Doctorate of Arts in Music Theory and Composition. Not only that, I had a full-time job waiting for me in South Carolina as a tenure-track professor. I had even acquired a great little cat named Twister who I completely adored, which was odd because I hated cats. Clearly, "Doctor" Akkerman had evolved.

CHAPTER 17: A PIANO DUDE'S GOTTA HAVE HOBBIES

NOBODY GETS TO KNOW ahead of time what their total count will be. Mine turned out to be eighty-five.

As a youth, my last race on a BMX track was probably 1981 in southern California. I saw all the big names come through for the national-level events: guys like Stu, Heary, Toby, PK, and Tinker. They were only teenagers then but loomed like Titans to my worshiping young eyes.

I did pretty well at the local tracks, but when I went up against nationally ranked experts like Eddie King and "Pistol" Pete Loncharovich, the limitations of my skills were revealed. I decided girls liked musicians more than dusty, fringe-sport bike jockeys, so I turned in my Torker-brand ride for a Fender-Rhodes keyboard and moved on.

Decades later in the summer of 2008, there was an article in the Spartanburg, South Carolina newspaper about a large-scale BMX race being held just a couple miles from my home. I thought it would be fun to revisit my childhood sport, so off I went to the local track to watch the kids and their dads tear it up.

I could hardly contain my shock at what BMX had become over the years. Everything had gotten bigger—the jumps, the corners (called "berms"), the starting hill, and the trophies. It seemed like every ten-year-old on the track had mastered technical maneuvers we had never even imagined in the late 1970s. "They call it manualing," the proud poppa sitting next to me said, referring to his son's speed-saving technique over the multiple jumps on the second straightaway. "Whatever they call it," I thought to myself, "I wanna do this!"

A couple months later I had my racing license with the American Bicycle Association, full race gear, and a new "cruiser" BMX bike with a killer zebra paint job. With my heart pounding like the intro of Van Halen's "Panama," I was on the starting hill hearing, "Okay riders, let's set 'em up—On the gate—Riders ready—Watch the lights" and BANG! the gate dropped. Everybody took off down the opening straight and by the first corner I was already in last place.

The results in my second and third qualifying heats (called "motos") were the same. I didn't transfer out to the day's final race (called a "main") against guys I thought looked slow when I had previously watched from the stands. I quickly learned that my having a big cardio-engine from years of mountain and road biking doesn't win races—it's all about maintaining speed over the obstacles and having the guts to not touch the brakes.

Watching, reading, asking, listening, and riding, I began teaching myself everything I could about the present-day version of BMX. I recorded the gate cadence and listened to it in the car. I scoured YouTube for "how to" videos. I started lifting weights and eating healthier. Even though I wasn't winning races, I started making main events and finishing consistently near the front. Based on my steady improvement, I committed to finishing top three in South

Carolina based on total points for the year and planned a racing itinerary for the rest of the season.

Every week, I hit the single-point events at the Carolina local tracks in Spartanburg, Greenville, and Charlotte. When regional races offered more points, I headed out for three- and four-hour drives to Ducktown, Bradley, Atlanta, Raleigh, and Sylacauga. When I went to Ohio to visit family, I brought my bike and raced in Dayton, Kettering, and Hamilton. In the summer, I took a road trip from South Carolina to Colorado and planned the entire route around big events I could hit along the way. I competed in four Tennessee races, three in the shadow of the Rocky Mountains, and three more in Topeka. Even though I'd been on the road for weeks and was running low on cash, food, and proper hygiene, I took a longer trek home through Atlanta to pick up one more race.

At the Atlanta race, I managed to infuriate one of the competitors who I had cut off coming out of a corner. He crashed off the course rather than bang elbows with me. His post-race anger only meant one thing to me—I had arrived! I was now good enough to be seen as a threat.

Racing against tough competitors all over the country paid off. In my South Carolina points competition, I moved into a close battle for first place with a crafty opponent, and the two of us put ourselves out of reach of the pack.

About this time, I began feeling pretty good about my rising abilities on the bike, but I noticed a couple unplanned benefits: I'd lost about twenty pounds and felt healthier than I had in years. But the best part is I'd made some really good friends. Seeing many of the same faces all over the region, I began to realize I was part of a tribe brought together for a common cause—racing a bike or cheering for someone who is. I noticed people remembering my name, sharing glimpses into their lives, and taking a genuine interest in mine. What a great sport I'd re-discovered.

In August, I raced my first national-caliber event in Raleigh and although I didn't make the podium, I overcame a peculiar, unexplained swelling in my left leg and qualified for the main all three days. Considering this was only my rookie year racing as an adult, I felt these were pretty good results. Around this time, I even broke ahead to first place in SC points and planned a major effort to keep that position.

I'd attended six Red Line Cup qualifiers (a regional series for the southeastern states) over the previous months and was stoked to head to the three-day series final in Garner, North Carolina, with one national-level event already under my belt. Friday night's race went okay. I made the main and managed third place over-all but knew the real competition would arrive the next morning and stay through Sunday.

Saturday's race was TOUGH. There were enough entries to break us into two groups and mine was stacked with guys I knew were usually well above my skill set. Coming out of the first berm I was in a good position and told myself to really pour it on—pedal with everything I can for the next jump! But nothing came out of my legs. They just turned the cranks with feeble effort as the competition rode away. Second moto, same thing—no power at all coming out of the corners, and I finished last. Just before the third moto I screwed up my nerves and said to myself, "You are NOT here to finish last. Now man-up and PEDAL you flippin' wimp!" Somehow, I managed to finish ahead of one guy and that was just enough—I was in the final.

When the gate for my main moto dropped there was no sound of glorious trumpets, no legions cheering my name, no maidens throwing flowers at my feet: only the sight of my haggard and beaten body rolling over the finish-line in last place. Defeated in mind and body, I decided there was no point in staying over for Sunday's event just to be summarily eliminated. I packed up the truck and headed home.

♦ ♦ ♦

I started to ponder if the swelling in my leg was more serious than I wanted to admit. I hadn't suffered any injury and yet the problem wouldn't go away. I decided to get checked out and from the moment I arrived at the medical center things happened crazy fast.

There was a blur of people and electronic equipment. Statements of concern came at me fast. "The leg doesn't look right; you need an ultrasound right now." "Whoa, I haven't found a vein yet without a clot." "DO NOT get off of that bed; we'll get you checked right into the hospital." "With deep vein thrombosis this extensive you're a good candidate for a surgical procedure." "The good news is you've responded well from the surgery; the bad news is you have a clot-causing genetic mutation and will need to be on anti-coagulant drugs and wear pressure stocking for the rest of your life." "The other good news is this drug will keep you from getting future clots that could break off, cause a stroke and kill you. The other bad news is that because of this drug you have to give up any physical activity that could cause external or internal injuries."

And with those words, my life as a competitive cyclist was over. The risks are too great, so I will never race again. This beautiful sport full of wonderful people had welcomed me in, allowed me to excel, given me a sense of accomplishment, improved my health, blessed me with new friendships, and now...I'm relegated to being the guy who watches from the stands and says, "Yeah, I used to race."

On a bad day, I feel sorry for myself and look at my bike with anger as I pass it in the neglected corner of the garage. Cycling has been a part of every decade of my life and a major component of my identity. Although my friends mean well with their suggestions, just how am I supposed to "take up a new hobby like golf" when I've known the thrill of busting out of the gate, clearing a double jump, manualing through the rollers, and nailing an opponent right at the finish?

On a good day, I ask myself, "If an angel came down and said I could have all the joys of BMX racing, the excitement, the improved self-image, the fellowship, everything...but only for a specific number of races, and then I'd forever have to give it up...would I agree to it?" Of course, the answer is, "In a frickin' heartbeat. Where do I sign?" Well, that number turned out to be eighty-five. There's no reason for me to think it will ever go higher, but it was worth it, absolutely, no doubt about it.

Age 43 in South Carolina

CHAPTER 18: IN THE SLAMMER FOR JANET JACKSON

IF ONLY I HAD WOKEN UP EARLIER that summer morning in the desperate throes of projectile diarrhea, then everything would have ended up much cleaner. But I stayed in bed sleeping comfortably while Venessa got up and began her day ahead of mine, and thus was my fate of six months of court-ordered anger management classes sealed.

I have no idea exactly what she went through in my absence that morning. I never asked and never shall. I'm sure it wouldn't make things clearer. But the facts reveal the following: she DID get the newspaper from the driveway; she DID open it up to at least the entertainment section; she DID take a pair of scissors and cut out a rectangle from the upper-left corner of page D-16; and she DID close the paper nicely and leave it on the table where I would be likely to take my turn perusing the bits within.

I soon stumbled along to find my way to the kitchen. In retrospect, it was odd that Venessa made herself scarce upon my arrival. It was more common that we hung out together in the morning playing three games of Yahtzee (therefore always having a clear victor in our ongoing board-game wars). "Fair enough," I thought. It would allow me to read the paper at a casual pace—something not really possible if we both sat at the breakfast table together. Indeed, that act had been the source of ongoing angst in our two years of cohabitation. I didn't think it rude to have the paper open during breakfast and use it as a catalyst for conversation, and at first, she tried to accommodate. But the level of tension it seemed to put on her was palpable, as if she were being ripped apart by vicious inner-dialogues making her willing to attack anyone within, say, the distance of a breakfast table. I soon stopped the practice and would save the paper for later in the day.

But not that morning. No, I sat down with my usual victuals of spoon-sized shredded wheat and placed the paper in front of me. Like many people do, I first glanced across the top-of-the-fold headlines but found nothing of great importance and so moved on. It wasn't until getting to page D-15 in the entertainment section that I found something interesting—a 3x5-inch piece of nothing where something blacker and whiter should have been. I immediately assumed Venessa must have found an article so intriguing that she clipped it out for future reference, but it didn't match up to the story boxes on the current page so I flipped it over to see what might have been removed.

A bold-print headline stated "Unfortunately, Sex Sells and Talent Sinks." The article bemoaned the current state of celebrity status in the world of R & B/hip-hop, but the accompanying photo was missing. "Hon!" I called out, "What's the deal with the paper?" Coming in from the other room, Venessa planted herself near me in a standing position and pronounced what was clearly a rehearsed and anticipated statement: "There was a trashy picture there of Janet Jackson that I don't want you seeing so I got rid of it." That's when things got mighty interesting.

This kind of controlling censorship had been a bizarre problem in our relationship and unlike anything I had ever encountered. The only hint of this issue to appear during our early dating was when we were watching an episode of "Friends." It was the one where someone made a pithy comment with sexual overtones while sitting at the coffee shop. Remember that one? I chuckled at the scene. She scowled. When I pressed her, she said, "I'm uncomfortable viewing adult content" which I found surprising considering "Friends" was some pretty mild stuff by my standards.

I should interject that when I first started dating Vanessa, she was a delight. Her many attributes included optimistic energy, vast talent, and old-school charm. During the bulk of our time together, she was a fun person to be around at least 51% of the time. That's what kept me in the relationship: hope that the 49% would diminish to an even quieter minority—alas, the math fell the other direction.

Anyway, back to the "Friends" moment. Only much later did I postulate that what she really meant was, "*I'm* fine seeing adult content, but I'm horribly uncomfortable when *you* see adult content." In the course of our relationship I was inundated with accusative questions like: "Why do you always have to look at the magazine covers in the supermarket lines?" "Why do you always take the path through the Walmart that goes through the lady's underwear?" "Why are most your CDs of women?" "Why did you tip the female waitress so much?" "Will you promise me you'll never think of ex-girlfriends again?" "Will you please always look away from the TV anytime partial nudity is shown?" "Will you promise me not to look at the Victoria's Secret storefront even when I'm not with you?"

Sometimes I agreed with little discussion. Sometimes I fought vehemently for the principal involved—specifically, why should I pay a price for some form of perceived deviant misbehavior I had not committed? Eventually, I simply refused to even acknowledge such baggage-loaded questions. I determined that she was the victim of a lifetime of indoctrination and/or chemical imbalance that had no relationship to my real-world actions, and I would no longer be her enabler. That was the current state of affairs by the time we got to our breakfast with the absent Ms. Jackson.

"Are you completely insane?" I asked with a raised and serious voice. She promptly responded with, "I won't allow that kind of pornography in our home." Knowing that the family-friendly newspaper in our small city was not going to publish a photo more than PG-rated, I came back with, "Right. I'm sure Janet's got her bare tits and ass just stickin' in the camera!" That triggered some rapid escalation of tensions for Venessa. Me referring in any way to another woman's sexuality was difficult for her. She started to tremble as the anxiety wormed through her body.

"Where are you going?" she nervously implored as I grabbed my wallet and keys. With intense calm right on the verge of eruption, I said, "I'm going to go buy a newspaper that hasn't been sanitized by you for my protection." She moved quickly ahead of me and blocked my access to the doorway. That kind of maneuver and been a major issue for us in previous arguments and we had often talked about it in post-trauma debriefings when we attempted to better understand each other.

She so hated the idea of being abandoned that she would use her body as a desperate attempt to keep me from leaving mid-argument. I, on the other hand, considered blocking a doorway an act of aggression that was borderline imprisonment. I had previously let her know, "I am a grown up and forcing me to stay in a room to is not okay. If you block a door, I WILL MOVE YOU."

Using my chest, I pushed my way out the front door. She cried after me down the walkway, "Please, don't buy that paper. YOU CAN'T DO THAT TO ME!" She raced by me to again use her body as a barrier to my opening the car door. With increased aggression, I once more moved her aside and quickly slid behind the steering wheel. She dove in after to keep me from inserting a key into the ignition, and I stopped trying for a moment to consider my options. She stood within the open door, and even if I could get the engine started, I would not have been able to back out the driveway without the car rolling her down. I knew how stubborn we could be. There would be no compromise. I would under no terms argue about whether or not I had the right to an uncensored newspaper, and she would under no terms allow me to leave in the middle of a fight.

I decided to logically explain what I was going to do next as a final plea and warning. With a steady, clear voice, I said, "If you don't move and allow me to leave, I am going to have no choice but put my foot on your stomach and push you back out of the way." She looked me dead in the eye and made another stabbing reach for my keys, so I carried out my threat.

Just as described, I set the bottom of my shoe against her gut and gave a push. In the midst of this horrible action I wimped out and only succeeded in causing her to lose her balance and fall down rather than sending her flying back several feet as I might have. She attempted to steady herself by grabbing the car door but caught her thumb on an edge and ended up tearing a cuticle, resulting in a few drops of blood. Having not succeeded in completely dislodging her, I realized I would not be able to leave and gave up. The rest of the day was spent in cold silence.

That was the only way I could process those kinds of moments. Our relationship had become such an absurd situation that if I wasn't allowed to physically leave (she would threaten to kill herself), I just mentally left the premises. I would lay on the bed and simply go away in my head. I would travel the world to beautiful, peaceful environs surrounded by butterflies that danced through rainbows to the sounds of exotic Latin-piano rhythms. On this particular occasion, Venessa left for a couple hours, and upon her return, no explanation was asked or offered.

As the evening progressed, I hesitantly turned on the TV to fill the living room with distraction. This was usually not tolerated in the aftermath of an argument with Venessa's logic being that until I apologized, I was not entitled to any activity that resembled fun. But much to my surprise, she let me be, just as she had the entire afternoon. I wondered if her willingness to allow me space was an unspoken admission that her morning actions had indeed been unwarranted. For the moment, I had forgotten just what a fireball of chaos I had partnered with.

There was a firm knock on door that startled me up from the sofa. An unexpected visitor after 10 p.m. was entirely unusual, so I approached the door with slight apprehension. I saw Venessa down the hall with a look that displayed no surprise at all. Looking through the front-door glass I could make out badges and uniforms on a duo of Sheriff officers. I assumed something must have happened at one of the neighbors, and they were coming around to ask if we'd seen anything. One of them asked for me by name. "That's me," I replied, still believing I was about to serve as a helpful citizen. "Sir, we have a warrant for your arrest for Felony Domestic Violence. You're going to have to come with us."

Venessa had moved closer to see the look on my face at the moment of my realization that she had been playing me all day long. I had disagreed with her, and that simply wasn't allowed by someone with her issues. I had given her weapons to wield against me, and she couldn't stop herself. Soon, I was in the back of the cruiser and on my way to the county jail for a sleepless night of processing, oral-sex offers, courtroom judgements, and bail bondsmen.

Like many male musicians my age, I thought Ms. Jackson was fine as wine, but damn it Janet, you ain't jail-time fine.

ENDNOTE:

I wish I could say that the day described here was unique, but it was just one of hundreds filled with her bizarre, irrational, and dangerous behavior. She was never officially diagnosed, but a social worker and two relationship therapists (one with a doctorate) all suggested the same thing: Borderline Personality Disorder. This is one nasty mental disorder with a litany of horrid symptoms and little hope for improvement.

Our relationship lasted several years and was ultimately the source of great anguish, but its necessary demise marked a return to my previously awesome life. I include this chapter not as a means to be dramatic or judgmental but as a warning. If you read through this account and think, "That sounds like the same situation I'm in," I have one all-encompassing suggestion for you that I wish to God someone had given me:

Leave.

CHAPTER 19: JOHNNY HARTMAN AND BILL COSBY

MANY YEARS AGO, I WAS RIDING IN A CAR to a jazz concert with a few musician cohorts when "Lush Life" from the iconic *John Coltrane and Johnny Hartman* album began playing on the stereo.

"I heard everything on the album was recorded in one take," said my friend in the driver's seat.

"You know, Johnny Hartman was only 17 when he joined up with Earl Hines," said another.

Still one more passenger chimed in, "Hartman never got more famous because he spent most of his career overseas."

The conversation then waned into silence before rebooting into a 30-minute discourse on the merits of John Coltrane's use of exotic scales and modes. That summed up nicely the situation for Hartman. There he was, the beloved vocalist on one of the most important vocal jazz records ever made, and all he elicited from our group of ardent jazz fans was three brief comments—and all incorrect comments at that. Coltrane has been studied and dissected down to the specific transcription of nearly every note and quote ever put on record. But what of the only singer ever to be featured on a Coltrane album?

Hartman had somehow escaped the glare of journalistic and popular scrutiny since his death in 1983 from lung cancer. In 1995, his career enjoyed a posthumous spike in popularity following the use of his recordings in Clint Eastwood's *The Bridges of Madison County*, but at the time, the press reported on him in near mythical terms using only one or two error-ridden articles as sources. Hartman was described in ghostly, beyond-human terms which superseded reliance on the earthly reality that he might have merely been a man who worked hard, walked his daughters to school, passed out business cards displaying his home number, and had a wife with a day job.

Hartman had become more legend than man, and legends don't need to have their stories straight. Within the liner notes for each new album reissue, his story got increasingly vague. The same few quotes were regurgitated and sometimes even mutated, making their next appearance still further removed from the original intent. Suppositions reported as fact became fodder for the next writer unwilling to check the source material. Legends don't need inconvenient details to get in the way.

And now, after several decades of mostly inadvertent mythologizing, even Hartman fans with the best of intentions don't really know anything about the man they so adore when hearing his "My One and Only Love," "I'll Remember April," or "I See Your Face Before Me."

I decided in early 2010 to clarify Hartman's legacy and document the story while I could still track down enough of his family, friends, and peers. The resultant book, *The Last Balladeer: The Johnny Hartman Story* (Scarecrow Press "Studies in Jazz" series) is the result of two years' work, and worth every minute to me. For music fans not overly familiar with Hartman's music or life, a brief version of his story can be told through some of the quotes culled from the many interviews I conducted for the book.

Several of the greatest vocalists in classic pop and jazz cite Hartman as an influence and friend. For example, singer Bill Henderson spent the end of his life still making great music in southern California, but told me what it was like to hear Hartman sing back home in late-1940s Chicago: "I knew Johnny when he first started out and Larry 'Good Deal' Steele introduced him at a club in Chicago....He was tremendous and the women in the crowd went crazy." In a later conversation, Henderson told me he was impressed how Hartman didn't need to overplay physical gestures because his voice was pure enough to grab the audience's attention without staged histrionics that other singers used as a crutch.

At age 90 when I interviewed him, vocalist legend Jon Hendricks was still a great admirer of Hartman, but reminded me of a problem all male, black singers faced during the late 1940s and early 1950s—getting compared to the fabulous Billy Eckstine. Referring to Hartman, Hendricks said, "He was plagued, I would say, by the Billy Eckstine onset. Eckstine hit town, man, and everybody had to take a back seat.... Hartman was in his shadow, and that was a hell of a big shadow." Hartman persevered through this racially convenient comparison to develop a singular style and decades later, it is Hartman rather than Eckstine that gets more airplay on jazz radio stations.

In 1955, Hartman was given the opportunity to record his first long-playing album for Bethlehem Records, an independent label that was moving away from pop towards jazz. They placed him with an excellent jazz combo led by the young, unproven pianist, Ralph

Sharon, who blew me away with his vivid memories of the one and only time he and Hartman ever worked together all those years ago. He told me, "Okay, you know I was with Tony Bennett for forty years, and I've made my living as an accompanist, and I'll tell you something; that Hartman—I've never forgotten it—that's the best voice I've ever heard on a male singer." These are the kinds of comments that make me realize just how highly Hartman was and is regarded by those he worked with.

As for Tony Bennett himself, he was nice enough to tell me that "Johnny Hartman is one of the greatest singers of all time." I sent Bennett a copy of the book, and shortly after he was on the *George Stroumboulopoulos* TV show in Canada where he was asked to name a singer that should have been more popular. Without pause Bennett replied, "Johnny Hartman was the best singer I ever heard. Jazz artists knew him, [and] that was about it. But when you hear his records, you can't believe it."

It was a quote from Johnny himself that best communicated the melancholy reality he applied to his own career that simmered just below mainstream popularity. During my many conversations with Hartman's widow, Tedi, she shared with me something her husband once said: "I have a feeling my work won't be appreciated until after I'm gone." This was indeed the case. Hartman's legacy has grown substantially since his premature death through outlets like Bridges, his songs being used in Victoria's Secret commercials and hour-long TV dramas, and finally, his own biography.

To me, Hartman has grown to represent the very voice of romance in our times. The unadorned, molasses-sweet, sanguine tone of his baritone voice transcends the years to share stories of love and hope in a century he never saw and yet perfectly understood. He knew love would still fill our dreams, and hope would still keep us searching for that very love we crave. Hartman died all too young at the age of sixty, but the secrets to life were already his, and we can hear about it anytime one of his ballad recordings reaches our ears.

I consider the writing of "The Last Balladeer: The Johnny Hartman Story," my supreme academic achievement and one of the more lasting of my accomplishments. The entire process—researching, interviewing, writing, and traveling the country for guest lectures and book signings—was an act of joyful creativity. As Tony Bennet has often said, "Do what you love and you'll never work a day in your life." I'm trying Tony, I'm trying.

Amazing People I Interviewed

I was incredibly fortunate to interview dozens of Hartman's associates, bandmates, family members, and friends. This is especially true because many of them have died since the interviews. Bill Henderson, Jon Hendricks, Ralph Sharon, Billy Taylor, Tony Monte, Marion VerPlanck, and several others—all gone now.

But the most awkward interview I conducted was with none other than **Bill Cosby**.

The Hartman family loves to recount the story of Johnny bringing home a young, unknown comic for dinner one night in the early 1960s. Cosby, with his wife Camille, graciously spent an evening with the Hartman family enjoying a homecooked meal while on the road.

This family legend grew over the decades, and by the time I came along, Johnny and Bill were "old friends and comrades." I eventually determined that beyond that one occasion, the two men likely never interacted with each other again. Unlike today's celebrities "throwing shade" at each other for social media attention, entertainers of Johnny's era usually spoke as if every peer was their "closest pal" even if they barely knew each other.

But, not knowing better at the time, I tracked down a phone number for Bill Cosby through an editor at a Chicago newspaper, and I assumed it was for a management office. I called the number on a Sunday afternoon expecting voice mail to reveal who the number belonged to.

As you have probably guessed, Bill Cosby himself answered the phone. There's no mistaking the voice I grew up hearing on TV as Fat Albert and his gang, Mr. Huckstable, and the pudding-pop guy.

Clearly, I had dialed his home phone, and Cosby was in the middle of watching a football game. Caught off guard, I stammered my way through an introduction and explanation for my call. Something like, "Bla-blah, babble, blah, Johnny Hartman, blah-babble."

The good news was, he didn't hang up. The bad news was, he provided no help whatsoever. What followed was 15 minutes of me trying to get him on the record saying something about Hartman and him sidestepping my every effort.

I eventually tired of his deflections and asked him outright for a quote to use in the book regarding his opinions of Hartman's music. He quickly shot back in a stern, reprimanding tone, "Son, we are *not* going there!"

Feeling roundly scolded by one of TV's greatest father figures, I said my goodbyes and hung up. Whew! He was tough customer. You can bet I will never refer to him as my "closest pal."

As I write this paragraph years after the conversation occurred, I spent the day on a beautiful beach in Honduras. Mr. Cosby sits in jail for drugging a woman to have sex with against her will.

CHAPTER 20: REPETITION

HE CRAVED NUMBERS. They allowed the illusion of subtle structure in a universe of random foofaraw. He knew better, but convinced himself anyway. He was a professional pianist and by some accounts, could have been a classical prodigy. But there was that unpleasantness at the age of twelve when he was scolded for tapping his foot while playing Beethoven. "Who wants to play music you can't tap your foot to?" he asked his un-amused teacher. No, he was a jazz and rock pianist. Here was his ultimate security. Here was his conclave. Here, the improvised notes only appear random to the untrained. But to him, it was the closest he could come to controlling the numbers, controlling the frequencies, controlling the neurons.

He arrived at his weekly gig and went through the checklist: enter the dining area with a shoulder pack full of music books; greet the employees with the friendly but detached smile ("I like you, but we'll never be very close"); open the piano lid and hope the guy from last night didn't leave another disgusting cigar butt on the keys (all clear); turn down volume on cell phone and set it nearby so the clock would remind him to take a break after exactly fifty minutes; take books out of bag, though he seldom used them; check over his song list to pick an opening tune (which always ends up being "Our Love Is Here to Stay"); and, finally, seated at the piano with wearied posture, place fingers on the instrument to begin.

But this night the ritual was broken, though no one but him cared to notice. The bartender was busy looking at an attractive customer; the waitress was looking at the bartender wishing he would look at her that way; and the couple seated near the piano looked only at each other across wine glasses. On this singular evening, the pianist deviated from the norm as his fingers drifted away from the keys and returned to the shoulder bag. Empty of its heavy books, it flaccidly revealed a weathered photograph: a color-faded Polaroid never meant to last so many decades. With a left hand barely suggesting a hesitant quiver, he lifted the photo and placed it in sight next to the phone.

The first song began and he commenced his beautiful-mind formulae. The ears in the room heard only the harmonically pleasing and technically impressive notes that fell from his seemingly effortless hands. But in his mind, the numbers churned and processed while seeking out purpose, order, and the perfect placement in series. The commentary flashed through his mind:

> *Sevenths resolve down; leading tones resolve up; Lydian dominant sounds exotically bluesy; borrowed chords add a touch of melancholy, don't overdo the chromatic scale (the coward's bitch); develop a three-note cellular theme and slightly abstract it for each of two more occurrences (not one, not three, TWO!); employ a different turn-around progression at the end of each chorus even though they are all just bastard children of the immortal original; a smattering of Bud, a whisper of Wynton, a nod to Duke, and an outright theft of Nat, before closing with 'Ending Number 28' from Hyman's big book of '101 Greatest Jazz Intros and Endings (With Chords Real Pros Use!).'*

These and a thousand other possibilities smashed through his brain until the song's conclusion. Non-musicians have no idea how messed up the mind of an engaged jazz musician is. The polite applause is acknowledged with a slight head bow, but no eye contact ("I'll give you all of my music, but not much else.").

No one noticed when the pianist stole a few more glances than normal towards his phone. The song list consulted. A second tune chosen. The numbers swim and dodge and flutter. The process is continued. Repetition is comfort. Repetition is home.

At some point in the midst of a song, he thinks back to when he played for a while in an oldies rock band. Solo piano suits him better. He finds group dynamics confusing and the odd quirks of others hurt his brain. He specifically remembers Gabby—a great singer but so hard to figure out. There was the one gig in particular that always perplexed the pianist. On that night, Gabby was strangely subdued before the first set as he sucked a long drag from his Marlborough, prompting the polite question, "What's up?" "Nothing," answered Gabby. "My brother's dying tonight. Family's gonna O.D. 'im on morphine." After an uncomfortable pause, one word is added: "Aids."

That didn't make any sense to the pianist. Aren't people supposed to stay home when someone dies? How selfish. Aren't there rules about that? Isn't singing "Splish, splash, I was takin' a bath," while your brother takes his last breath just wrong?

There in the restaurant, the songs continued. The evening played out. The calculations delivered their desired results. He was a jazz and rock pianist. And he was methodically good. On this night, he closed with Monk's "'Round Midnight:" a beast of a tune, but it allowed for the mathematically satisfying whole-tone scale, so the pianist was drawn to it. Coming out of the bridge in what would be the last chorus, his phone lit to a soft glow that caught his eye. The text message displayed only two words:

"He's gone."

The pianist returned to the task at hand and prepared a delicate cadence melded from several different recordings he had studied over the years. At the last moment, he pulled his middle finger from the usual G and chose instead a G-flat. He let the final minor chord ring a touch longer than usual before releasing it to oblivion.

Then, the ritual occurred in reverse: phone volume up; books (not ever used) back in the bag; and piano lid shut. That's when the placement of the photo perplexed him. It's not normally there. Its existence was awkward. He picked it up and stared at the image: broad Teutonic nose, loud short-sleeved shirt, thick-rimmed black glasses like Dave Brubeck used to wear, and a slight smile that appeared friendly enough but not quite present.

"Goodbye Dad," said the pianist as he slid the photo into a pocket and walked towards the door.

And then, softly to himself, "Fuck you Gabby."

Repetition is good. Repetition is life. Repetition is.

CHAPTER 21: IF IT DOESN'T FIT IN THE VETTE, I DON'T NEED IT

BY EARLY SPRING 2012, I HAD ALREADY BEGUN CONTEMPLATING leaving my professor job in South Carolina. The urge started to gestate while I was on a sabbatical granted me to finish writing my Johnny Hartman book. The concept of being paid a decent salary while working considerably less time was addictive, to say the least.

This is a good time to mention some thoughts on being a college professor and what I learned being around academia. Overall, I enjoyed being in the classroom immensely. The students are usually there for the right reasons and respond to material when presented to them with sincerity and personal interest. Unfortunately, universities are in a terribly competitive world fighting for enrollment against other institutions. The result is that many students are accepted who really aren't ready for college. But they are enticed with financial aid packages comprised mostly of student loans that aren't clearly understood as "loans."

Time and again, I saw students flounder through several semesters, falling further behind in studies and further behind in debt. Ultimately, they don't graduate, have lost several years advancing in the work force, and owe thousands of dollars for a product they never benefited from. In my opinion, colleges are complicit in encouraging young people to enter into a cycle of failure and debt that is doing great harm to the very people they purport to care about. This was my growing realization about higher education in America, and I was looking for a way out.

With my diminishing job interest, and no spouse, children, or even a pet to keep me anchored to the area, I began to seriously consider how I might be able to move back home to California. I had a reasonable nest egg of cash and an advance coming my way for the next book, but I had to be careful of burning through those reserves too fast while waiting for a new gig to open up. Just when I started to think my escape might face at least a year's delay, I got the most remarkable offer from a family friend: "Hey Gregg, if you come to San Diego you can live on my sail boat docked at the Marriott for free while you write your book." Boom! I started prepping my house for sale the next day.

I drove my pickup truck to California just before Christmas using the southern interstates to avoid bad weather. I managed to pack all my music and camping gear and parked the loaded rig in my Mom's garage before flying back to Spartanburg to further prepare for the move.

I had been reading some blogs about living a minimalistic life and had already greatly reduced the clothes in my closet and the books on the shelf. But now faced with the actual process of moving a household full of stuff across the country, I got a crazy idea—what if I only take what I can fit in my Z06 Corvette coup? *Everything* else will be sold, given away, or trashed.

I went on a total bender of downsizing the amount of crap in my life. I became fully addicted to having less material content to weigh me down. I quickly realized that less stuff resulted in an abundance of freed-up mental bandwidth that could be put to use elsewhere. Every time a large item hit the bottom of the trash bin, it sounded like bells of freedom ringing victoriously. I came up with a process to determine what stayed in my life:

1. If the item is irreplaceable and something I have actually used in the last couple years, keep it.

2. If the item is something I use nearly every day and not too large, keep it.

3. If the item is irreplaceable and something I am deeply attached to even though I don't use it for anything, keep it.

4. Everything else is expendable and can be found, bought, borrowed, or viewed for free on the internet at a later date if I ever actually miss the original item.

What about photo albums? I scanned the pictures, put the originals in space-saving envelopes and tossed out a dozen large binders.

What about personal books? They are nearly all replaceable, many of them for free through the internet or libraries. And even if a book is truly irreplaceable, it doesn't mean it's worthy of being stored the rest of my life. I'll give it to someone else who can't get rid of their surplus belongings and know that I can always borrow it back from them.

Old records and CDs? They're all on YouTube or a cloud service somewhere. The originals are *nice* to have, but I don't truly *need* them when it comes down to it.

The secret I stumbled on was to downsize in layers—not all at once. I could look at a shelf of ten items and barely convince myself I could live without a couple of the items. Then, a few days later I'd revisit the same shelf and find that I could pick a couple more things to let go of. It would have been impossible for me to give up 4 items on the first try, but by doing it in layers, it was much more manageable.

I found this subject caused considerable friction for some friends and family as they saw me cull all my belongings down to a car load. It made them ponder their own garage full of boxes that hadn't been open since two moves ago. They were thinking, "My stuff is my identity. If I get rid of it, who am I?" All I can tell you is what I came to conclude for my life, and it doesn't have anything to do with you.

When I pulled out of South Carolina with my only possessions being what was piled in the immediate space around me, I had never felt so liberated. My friend Gabby joked that all I took with me were my wits and an iPad. I consider this act of minimalization to be one of the most important aspects of self-improvement I have ever completed, second only to my commitment to eating healthy and getting regular exercise.

With the Vette loaded and the engine rumbling, the next ten days were spent on nothing but country highways that roughly shadowed Interstate 40, including much of what remains of Route 66. With each of the 2,600 miles put behind me I felt a growing sense of empowerment and clarity. My original destiny that had been temporarily blocked was back on track and coming into focus. Windows down, music up—if felt damn good to be alive.

Age 47, road trip across the U.S. including Route 66

CHAPTER 22: MY LIFE IS A JIMMY BUFFETT SONG

"WOW, YOU ARE REALLY LIVING the dream life." I long ago lost track of how many times I've heard those words from friends, family, and complete strangers. But I won't deny they are true. I make good money, travel to exotic locations around the world for free, work with talented and attractive people, have food and lodging provided, receive medical care without being billed, spend my days relaxing in the equivalent of a high-class hotel resort, and hang out with friends every night being offered free drinks while hearing all my favorite songs. So yes, I see it for the dream life it is. I have the awesome job of being a Piano Bar Entertainer on cruise ships.

Part of my job is being continuously asked the same handful of questions by well-meaning guests and friends. It's time for me to just write it all down in one place and say, "read this," so I can save my voice for more important things like yelling, "Bomp-bomp-bom" in the middle of "Sweet Caroline" for the millionth time. So here it is, the gritty "behind the scenes" truth of the ship-life world I've created for myself, presented in convenient FAQ form.

How Did You Get Your Piano Bar Entertainer Job?

Several years ago, I visited a dueling piano bar in San Diego and was blown away at how much fun they were and how the song list is comprised of primarily pop and classic rock. I was living on a sailboat at the time, looking for a new direction because I was about to finish my book on Led Zeppelin, and thought, "How can I build on the idea of performing like those guys while still living on a boat?" Cruise ships were the obvious answer. I got my first gig through an agency and have since been able to book myself direct. My auditions are primarily based on videos I post on YouTube.

Do You Have Other Jobs Besides Music to Perform on the Ship?

No, but I do have to partake in regular safety training. I can often be heard to say that I have the best job on the ship, and when the actual hours I am on the clock are matched to the money I bring in and the general good times I have every night, I firmly believe it's true.

How Long Is Your Contract?

I try to select contracts about eight weeks long. I alternate this with eight weeks off the ships, which allows me to feel like I am still active in my home life and growth of the family. This schedule results in me usually working three contracts each calendar year, although I might pick up a short fill-in gig along the way.

Do You Live on the Ship the Whole Time?

Yes. It's not like there is a waiting room next door full of back-up piano bar entertainers for when I fly home in the middle of the week. I'm it, and if I go down with a cold, the piano bar closes for the night, so I try very hard to stay healthy. I make a pretty good daily salary whether I play or not, but the bar staff really count on tips as the bulk of their income. Cruise ships are not flagged in the U.S., so the minimum wage laws Americans are used to don't apply. Most guests have no idea their bar and wait staff might only be paid a salary of a few dollars a day. Tips mean everything to them.

Do You Work When You Are Home?

I don't have a conventional day-job at home and seldom perform in my local area. I have self-employed author and investment interests to maintain, but mostly I dedicate myself to life as a house husband by doing the shopping, cooking, errand running, dog walking, and being mostly ignored by my teenage step-daughter.

When this question comes up, I think the cheeky hidden meaning is, "Do you *really* make enough money to only work six months out of the year?" And the answer is, "yes," but that's because I worked very hard in previous years to get out of debt and pay cash for everything (thank you Dave Ramsey). Simply put, I am satisfied making less money than others might be in exchange for a lifestyle that allows me to only work six months out of the year.

What Does Your Wife Think of All This?

This is a fairly loaded question usually only asked by women in the piano bar. They seem to be evenly divided into those who would love the idea of their husbands being gone months each year, and those who think I'm a rascal for being away having "fun" while my poor wife is at home living a lonely, domestic life.

In other words, if my job was more "work," like the military or on an oil rig, that might be acceptable, but playing music doesn't qualify.

All I know is that my wife constantly shows her appreciation for me being a good earner who loves her madly and is TOTALLY present for the months I am home with her. I suspect she gets more care and attention than many wives whose husbands are right there on the sofa every day of the year.

Can Your Wife Cruise with You for Free?

No, but the crew discount is attractive. Being a school teacher, Kathy is able to cruise with me for multiple weeks in the summer and that makes the time apart much easier.

Do You Ever Get Sick of Playing the Same Songs?

You know that scene in the movie *Ground Hog Day* where Bill Murray wakes up every day to the radio playing "I've Got You Babe?" That's pretty much my life in the piano bar.

Every night I get hit with a dozen requests in the first 10 minutes for "Piano Man," "Brown Eyed Girl," "Don't Stop Believing," "Friends in Low Places," "Sweet Caroline," and "Living on a Prayer." It's amazing how consistent the guests can be. But I totally get it—you're on vacation and those are the songs that *feel* right in a piano bar. You've been saving money all year and planning for your big escape to exotic destinations, so of course you think "Margaritaville" sounds like a good idea.

Here's the deal; you go right ahead and keep asking for those same tunes, and I'll keep right on playing them with a smile, but it's proper to include a healthy tip with your request. It shows respect for craft of live entertainment and makes the tedium more tolerable.

What Song Do You Hate to Play the Most?

At this point of my life, I have a rule that I simply won't play songs I hate. When such songs are requested, I say, "I don't know that one" and move on. I try not to be judgmental about it because I understand that a song I may not like might be incredibly meaningful to others.

That said, my version of hell is being trapped in a karaoke bar for eternity with an endless line of singers all taking a crack at "Music of the Night" from Andrew Lloyd Weber.

How Can You Keep Singing Night After Night and Not Lose Your Voice?

Constant effort and vigilance. The single biggest step I have taken is to not drink alcohol when I'm on the ships. This often surprises guests because they have seen other piano bar entertainers drink to excess. I choose not to live my life that way.

Also important is that I do a 30-minute vocal warm up every night before my show. After a month or two of performing up to four hours a night, six nights a week, these warm ups are critical to the strength of my voice. In addition, I try to eat healthy, get enough sleep, stay hydrated, and work out most days in the gym.

How Do You Fill Your Time During the Day?

Mostly by writing books like this one. I also learn 3-5 new songs every week, write an email every day to my wife, keep up on news and politics, hit the gym, and walk around the beautiful ports the ship visits. It's amazing how easy it is to find quiet moments on a cruise ship even with thousands of guests coming and going.

What Are the Crew Areas Really Like?

I get my own cabin that is small but serviceable. There are multiple dining halls with plenty of food selections. Human Resources regularly provides special events just for the crew like sports, parties, movie nights, bingo, and shore excursions. There is a crew bar where the drinks are cheap and the talk is free. But as an entertainer, I have full access to guest areas of the ship, so I'm not limited to where I spend my off time.

Like the chapter title says, my life is like a Jimmy Buffett song with a fancy umbrella in my drink and my feet in the sand. How did I get here? All it took was decades of effort, the love and support of the right life partner, a little luck, and the balls to say, "Yeah, I've got this" when the opportunity presented itself.

What Are the Strangest Things You've Seen?

Yup, I've seen some shit. Here are some of the highlights that come to mind.

--A creepy guy exposed himself to the whole bar while I played "My Ding-a-ling." It wasn't just a quick fling. We're talking full rotating swing motion for several seconds.

--A couple gals took off their bras and tossed them on the piano while I played a song called "Show Them to Me."

--I saw a lady so drunk she literally pissed herself in the chair she sat in. That night I learned cruise ships have a special cleaning crew that emerges after guests have gone to bed, and they sop up all the human goo and odors left behind.

--Unknown to me until later, someone had a seizure and split their head open just outside the piano bar, and I kept playing "Joy to the World (Jerimiah Was a Bullfrog)" while he almost died.

--I've had more boobs shaken in my direction by their owners than I can count.

--I've been grabbed, fondled, kissed, and groped by men and women, all without consent or enjoyment on my part.

--I've played through both proposals and breakups and watched guests applaud either way.

--Many times, I've played a request that resulted in the requester rushing out of the room in a crying fit. Why do people request songs they know will rip them apart? Please stop it.

--A guy tip me $1,000 in one night. He came to the piano bar a few nights later and tipped me a further $700. He didn't share any personal information beyond his first name, and I never saw him again.

What's the most memorable moment?

A sweet, elderly woman walked up to me at the piano and asked, "Would you please play the old song, 'Smile,' for me?" It's a pleasant song written by Charlie Chaplin with a slightly melancholy lyric. "Of course," I replied. Afterwards, she gave the biggest smile and said, "I used to sing that to my husband when we first dated over 50 years ago. Thank you so much for playing it." I acknowledged her and continued on with my show.

Later that night, the lady's husband told me, "My dear wife has Alzheimer's disease and most days she doesn't remember much, including me. It breaks my heart. But you played that song, and for the last hour I had my wife back. She knows me! We laughed and talked just like when we were young and so in love. You've given me a gift that can never be measured. Thank you, with all my heart."

I just about broke down. But there was more to come.

The next night of the cruise, that dear lady approached the piano and asked, "Do you know the old song 'Smile?'"

She had no memory of the previous night.

I gave her a cheerful look and happily agreed.

Just like the night before, the two wizened lovers became young at heart for a brief time right there in front of me. They even danced, while the husband tried to hide his tears. As did I.

And the next night...and the next...and the next...five nights in a row: "Can you play 'Smile' for me?" Five nights in a row I happily obliged with a lump in my throat. Each night she came to life in her husband's jubilant company.

I'm choking up just writing these words. It was the most beautiful of love stories, and I saw it play out five times.

My life is indeed charmed, and so good, so good, so *very* good.

SIDE NOTE:

If you or someone you know would like to learn everything involved with acquiring and keeping a cruise-ship musician gig, I wrote an entire book on the subject called "How to Be an Awesome Piano Bar Entertainer on Cruise Ships."

CHAPTER 23: A NIGHT IN A CRUISE SHIP PIANO BAR

I SURVEY THE ROOM while tinkling on the piano keys. Chat up the retired college educators from Pennsylvania and share I used to be a professor. Offer a friendly nod to the pleasant Corvette-owning couple that has come in every night and knows I have a Z06. Give a wink to the Captain's teenage daughter sailing with us this week who quickly flashes her brace-filled smile at me: she'll be a knock out in years to come. Welcome by name the husband-wife from South Carolina who I stopped near the pool earlier to reveal I had learned a song request just for them. Take a moment to connect with the two 40-something wives whose husbands have moved on to the casino. Observe the young-ish couple sitting in the dark corner sweetly holding hands. Take note that the big spender from Kansas isn't in yet, but he likes to make an entrance later in the night. Oh yeah, these and the other dozen people around the room make up a crowd I can work with.

Check the lights, adjust my hat, tip the microphone, and its business time.

"Ain't No Mountain High Enough" to start: a do-no-harm song that everybody likes but wouldn't likely request on their own. A piano bar entertainer never plays an A-list song without a request: don't waste the money makers.

While playing, I begin my routine of scan and smile.

Start to my far left. If it's a couple, always look at the lady first. Catch her eyes until she smiles, return the gesture and hold that moment just a second longer so she knows I really am looking at her, then move to her partner and give him a respectful "You're a lucky man" look.

Scan to the next group and start over. Older couple? Make sure I play some Elvis soon. College girls on spring break? Some Taylor Swift will have them gleefully singing along. The working man in a t-shirt and ball cap sitting with his 50-something wife who looks 65 from her years of hard decisions and cigarettes? Bob Seger and Tom Petty on the way.

Smile and scan.

A family reunion from Utah? I'll learn the name of the loudest and say, "Here comes trouble" when they bring up a request, making them all laugh with delight to think of themselves as rowdy.

Smile and scan.

The couple who dress exceptionally nice for their evening out? Clapton's "Wonderful Tonight" will do just fine as I say, "This one is for the ladies who put a little extra time into getting ready tonight." If the guy is smart, he'll ask her to slow dance and tip me for knowing I just got him some action later that night.

A 20th wedding anniversary shared with friends? A 30th birthday for a young mother free of the kids for a night? The solo hipster-guy who thinks I should play more obscure music he likes instead of popular music everyone else likes? Excellent.

Smile and scan.

I see you all. I acknowledge you all. While you sit here in front of me you have worth, you matter, you belong, and in another life, we would have been the closest of friends, lovers, siblings, soul mates and confidants.

Smile and scan.

A request for "Sweet Caroline" in the first five minutes? What a bold party animal you are. "Don't Stop Believing" is your favorite song? Of course it is, and no one has ever sung along about that small-town girl with as much conviction.

"Piano Man," you say? Well, I usually save that song for later, but you're such an awesome crowd that I'm going to break my rule and play it for you right now.

A $20 bill for playing the song I said I learned for you even though I already knew it? A $10 tip for keeping your wife occupied while you finished watching the game in your cabin? A $5 casino chip for playing "Joy to the World" a second time in 15 minutes? A $1 tip for a request slip with 10 songs on it? Requests for "anything Elton," "anything Adele," or "anything Billy Joel?"

Bring it on. I've got you covered good people.

"Please play YOUR favorite song?" Well, now we have a problem because I don't perform my favorite songs in public, but such details are inconvenient, so I'll break out "Let It Be" and we're good to go.

Then the questions come, as they always do. "Where are you from?" "How long are you here?" "And you live on the ship the whole time?" "You don't have a real job back home?" "Family?" "How does your wife feel about this?"

I elatedly provide answers because surely normal social boundaries don't apply to such intimate acquaintances as us.

When the evening concludes, I graciously accept platitudes as I gather my disco-ball sunglasses, feather boas, drink-splattered song lists, and crumpled dollar bills scattered across the piano lid.

"You are the best entertainer on the ship." "We've been on 7 cruises and you're our favorite piano man." "If only we'd found you sooner, we would have come every night." "Do you ever perform near Dayton?"

Always with sincerity I respond: Thank you; You are very kind; I really appreciate it; I'm sure it's very nice there.

And then there's the one who lingers because she's sure we've developed a bond over our several nights together.

It's been years since anyone has paid her as much attention, called her by name, told her she looks nice, and simply looked her in the eyes and smiled.

And my dear, you are right to want that, crave that, and finally receive that. If it feels special, then it is, and you can have that feeling forever if you choose. But it's late, the lights have dimmed, and it's time for me to leave.

Our evening was beautiful, joy-filled, and a rarity that may never be matched, but it was also just like any other night, and tomorrow it all starts over.

Check the lights, adjust my hat, tip the microphone...business time.

Except that one hour before showtime tonight I received a message my brother died alone in his truck parked behind a Taco Bell.

Do not ever play poker with me.

CHAPTER 24: 10 RULES FOR THE NEW WORLD DUDE

FOR SEVERAL YEARS NOW, I've been living the awesome life as the Piano Dude. It's been mostly terrific, and the regrets too few to mention. Yet even though I'll respond to, "Hey, Piano Dude!" the rest of my life, the time has come for yet more transition and expansion. Welcome the birth of the **New World Dude** and 10 rules to bring it all together.

I will be fearless in my career more often. Every time I am, I either victoriously succeed or gloriously fail, either way, I know I was fully committed and walking the bolder path.

I will open doors for women and tell them they look nice (not "sexy" or "hot") when it's true. If that's still sexist, then sexist I am.

I will keep voting in elections even though it seems that all politicians suck and most issues I favor lose. Democracy ain't for sissies.

I will earn my dog's love. Even though it's given unconditionally, it doesn't mean I deserve it.

I will keep my possessions lean. If I get a new shirt, an old one has to go. Stuff takes up mental bandwidth that I want available for "living the dream."

I will use the financial logic of any 10-year old and not spend money I don't have. Cash up front or not at all.

I will eat meat and wear leather without guilt. You might be able to sway me on various social issues, but this is not one of them.

I will respect my marriage by not joking with others about how awful the institution of marriage is. I hear men (and women) do this far too often. If it's a joke, it isn't funny. If it's actually true, then respect yourself and the person she might still become by manning up and moving on.

I will honor the life I've been given by choosing to keep my body in healthy condition. I don't know the ultimate point of life on earth, but I'd hate for it to be revealed the day *after* I die from something stupid I could have avoided.

I will find the grandest of pleasures in the simplest of moments: they are everywhere—just waiting for a smile.

***

To keep up with my adventures as a musician, follow my Facebook page at Piano Dude Gregg.

You can also download a **TOTALLY AWESOME LIFE-HACK FREEBIE** and find lots of interesting content at my blog: http://greggakkerman.com

ABOUT THE AUTHOR

Dr. Gregg Akkerman is a relationship expert, writer, and entertainer born in the southern California desert. He performed many years as a musician throughout the Southwest before earning a Master's Degree from San Diego State University and a Doctorate Degree from the University of Northern Colorado. He has authored **multiple #1 best-selling books** and is the founding editor of *The Listener's Companion* series from Rowman and Littlefield. After a decade teaching at a university as a tenured Associate Professor, Akkerman returned to California to marry his childhood crush, write books, perform as a piano bar entertainer, and live an awesome life. Follow his Facebook page at Gregg the Writer.

Author Gregg Akkerman
(photo by Don Emmanuel de Vera)

REQUEST FOR REVIEW

If you enjoyed this book and found it useful, I'd be very grateful if you'd post an honest review. Your support matters as I do read all the reviews and make changes based on your feedback.

If you'd like to leave a review, all you need to do is go to the book's Amazon page. Scroll down to the Customer Review area and you'll see a button/link that says "Write a customer review" – click on that and you're good to go.

Once again, if you're reading the e-Book, please click here to leave a review.

Thank you for the support,
Gregg

OTHER BOOKS FROM GREGG AKKERMAN

For the most current list of all my books, please visit my Amazon Author Page and select "Follow."

The Keyboardist's Career Guide: *A 10-Step Plan to Your Dream Job in the Music Business*
A #1 Bestseller on Amazon. This is the premiere career guidebook written specifically for keyboardists by a musician/author who has successfully followed his own advice for decades. Includes over 50 career possibilities, contact information, and specific financial examples. **Book #1** in the ***Awesome Music is Your Business*** Series.

How to Be an Awesome Piano Bar Entertainer on Cruise Ships
A #1 Bestseller on Amazon. The only book of its kind that breaks down every step of this lucrative dream-job where you get paid a salary to play your favorite songs, travel the world in style, and make thousands of people smile while they hand you cash tips. **Book #2** in the ***Awesome Music is Your Business*** Series.

Experiencing Led Zeppelin: A Listener's Companion
Consider Akkerman the voice of expert knowledge whispering in your ear as you listen to the music of hard rock's greatest band. Every song

in the Led Zeppelin studio-record catalog is discussed. From "Black Dog," to "Stairway to Heaven," and "Whole Lotta Love," it's all here.

The Last Balladeer: The Johnny Hartman Story

You've heard Hartman's glorious baritone voice on the iconic *John Coltrane and Johnny Hartman* album as well as in Clint Eastwood's *Bridges of Madison County* movie, and now you can read Akkerman's exquisitely written biography about the balladeer's life and music. Nominated for **"Jazz Biography of the Year"** by the Jazz Journalists Association.

Embracing Masculinity: *The New Dating Rules for Classic Dudes Seeking Classy Women*

Gregg Akkerman provides **a definitive dating manual** for classic men looking beyond hook-ups. This isn't a "players" guide to getting laid. This is for stand-up Dudes ready to use **3 Pillars of Modern Dating Wisdom**: ***FIRST***, powerful male figures became toxic in the wake of the #MeToo movement. Akkerman explains how this has changed dating rules for the better. ***SECOND***, dating starts with FLIRTING, but exactly what is and isn't appropriate anymore? Akkerman shows you step-by-step. ***THIRD,*** you'll learn if women really prefer the rich, stylish, bad-boys and how regular Dudes can compete. **Book #1** in the ***Men's Advice for New World Dudes*** Series.

Dating Your Wife: *A 10-Date Plan to Reignite Your Marriage as an Awesome Husband*

Gregg Akkerman provides a ***complete*** **dating manual** with specific blueprints for husbands wanting to reinvigorate their marriage and spice things up. This isn't a phony "quick fix" guide. It's for stand-up Dudes ready to implement a solid **Dating Action Plan**. You'll be shown thorough details for 10 completely unique dating blueprints including real-world examples from Akkerman's own experience.

There're also 10 invaluable answers to the most pressing questions husband face like, "Does my wife fantasize about leaving?" Lastly, you'll be provided scheduling suggestions and a dating Action Plan template certain to impress your wife. **Book #2** in the ***Men's Advice for New World Dudes*** Series.

Divorced and Dating: *The Dude's Guide to Starting Over and Attracting Wonderful Women*

Finally, a dating guide just for divorced men! Gregg Akkerman provides the *definitive* source for Dudes seeking to raise themselves up and become better men in the wake of a divorce. It's just that kind of Dude who wonderful women will find attractive. This is *not* a book about getting laid or being a victim after your divorce. It's about designing an *action plan* for dating and celebrating your potential. Think of Gregg as your older friend who cares deeply about your happiness but is totally willing to give you a head-smack if you're being a dumbass. **Book #3** in the ***Men's Advice for New World Dudes*** series.

Don't Stop Dating Your Lover: *A 10-Date Plan to Heat Up Any Committed Relationship*

Are you ready to ***add heat*** to your long-term relationship? **#1 best-selling author** Gregg Akkerman provides the *specifics* for 10 unique dating outlines to anyone ready to spice things up. This book is for lovers wanting to **maximize their passion** by continuing to date each other like when they first met. Each dating blueprint includes a *real-world example* from Akkerman's own experience. There are also 10 invaluable answers to questions people in long-term relationships face, such as, "Does my Partner fantasize about leaving?" You're also provided scheduling suggestions and a **Dating Plan** template that makes **dating your lover** even easier.

55018713R00083

Made in the USA
Columbia, SC
08 April 2019